CUTTING A NEW PATH

Donna T. Vande Kieft
5300 Glenwood Avenue
Unit K-1
Everett, WA 98203

CUTTING A NEW PATH

Helping Survivors of Childhood Domestic Trauma

LAURA DELAPLAIN

UNITED CHURCH PRESS
Cleveland, Ohio

United Church Press, Cleveland, Ohio 44115
©1997 by Laura Delaplain

From "A Service of Healing I" in the *United Methodist Book of Worship,* copyright © 1992 by the United Methodist Publishing House, used by permission. "The Cupped Hands Exercise" from the *Growing through Grief: Personal Healing* videocassette series used by permission of Howard Clinebell. Laurie Simon, page 71 in *Flames of the Spirit,* ed. Ruth C. Duck (1985), used by permission of The Pilgrim Press

Biblical quotations are from the New Revised Standard Version of the Bible, ©1989 by the Division of Christian Education of the National Council of the Churches of Christ in the U.S.A., and are used by permission.

All rights reserved. Published 1997

Printed in the United States of America on acid-free paper

02 01 00 99 98 97   5 4 3 2 1

Library of Congress Cataloging-in-Publication Data

Delaplain, Laura.
    Cutting a new path : helping survivors of childhood domestic trama / Laura Delaplain.
        p. cm.
    Includes bibliographical references (p.).
    ISBN 0-8298-1203-2 (pbk. : alk. paper)
    1. Adult child sexual abuse victims—pastoral counseling of.   2. Sexually abused children—Pastoral counseling of.   3. Child sexual abuse—Religious aspects—Christianity.   4. Pastoral counseling—Psychological aspects.   I. Title.
BV4464.3.D45   1997   97-33602
261.8'3273—dc21   CIP

To Donald Zook

Nathan and Joshua Delaplain-Zook

and James and Mary Kathryn Delaplain

Contents

	Acknowledgments	ix
	Introduction: Cutting a New Path	xi
1.	Identifying Victim-Survivors	1
2.	The Caregiver's Role	9
3.	Paradoxes of Value	19
4.	Myths of the Victim-Survivor	33
5.	Breaking the Silence, Telling the Story	46
6.	Confronting Wounders of the Past	59
7.	Exorcising Internal Haunters	72
8.	Recovering the Lost Child	81
9.	Restoring the Sacred	94
	Appendix: Sample Guided Meditations	108
	Notes	113
	Selected Bibliography	117

Acknowledgments

I acknowledge with gratitude the following people, who have encouraged and made possible the writing of this book:

For her redemptive pastoral counseling, Bonnie Niswander.

For his encouragement of my writing, Orlo Strunk.

For their feedback and ideas on my initial proposal, Bart Yates and Tim Ferreira-Bedard.

For her consultation and teaching, Linda Sanford.

For her supervision, Carole Bohn.

For her contribution of ideas, Barbara Hemmings Gray.

For their support, my colleagues and friends at the Norma Kent Pastoral Counseling Center, Beechwood Counseling Services, and the United Church of Christ in Abington, Massachusetts, especially Greg Carpenter, Tim Lanham, Jeanne Myett, Stan Duncan, and Deb Moore.

For the honor of letting me walk with them on their journey toward healing, my clients and parishioners who came from backgrounds of domestic trauma.

For his careful and caring review of the original manuscript, Jim Delaplain.

For their love, Donald, Nathan, and Joshua.

Introduction
Cutting a New Path

> I looked up the road I was going and back the way I come, and since I wasn't satisfied, I decided to step off the road and cut me a new path.
> —Maya Angelou, *Wouldn't Take Nothing for My Journey Now*

For survivors of childhood domestic trauma, the process of recovery from the emotional and spiritual wounding is life-encompassing yet life-sustaining. The healing process is a spiritual process, a spiritual path. This book addresses the challenges of the pastoral caregiver in facilitating healing with individuals recovering from wounds of the past, individuals who have stepped off the road of inherited dysfunction to cut a new path for themselves.

Many among us, perhaps all of us, carry pain from our childhood that gets in the way of our living the lives we would like to live in the present. Most of us know the feeling of hearing a parent's ignorant words or phrases come out of our own surprised mouths in moments of conflict or confusion, words we heard years ago and vowed to ourselves not to pass on. We know the sinking awareness of continuing to make the same mistakes in relationships or in important situations yet somehow feeling powerless to do or say differently, having little conscious choice about who we are in those moments. If we exponentially broaden these experiences that are common to most people, we have a taste for what many survivors of childhood abuse experience.

Quite a number of people among any community of faith carry a reservoir of pain that developed during prolonged childhood domestic trauma, trauma that would debilitate an adult, never mind a child. This reservoir of pain, whether felt or repressed, deeply disturbs an adult's capacity to experience life as a whole person, to possess a degree of life choice, to hold a sense of responsibility for oneself, and to be able to love and be loved.

Maya Angelou writes:

> Each of us has the right and the responsibility to assess the roads which lie ahead, and those over which we have traveled, and if the future road looms ominous or unpromising, and the roads back uninviting, then we need to gather our resolve and, carrying only the necessary baggage, step off that road into another direction.[1]

Recovery from childhood wounding entails stepping off the road into another direction. Many survivors say they don't want to pass the pain on to another generation.

CARE OF THE SOUL

The sources of childhood wounding are varied: all of our communities include adult survivors of childhood physical and sexual abuse, adults who were raised by alcoholic parents, adults who as children suffered unaddressed and unconsoled losses, and adults who as children simply lost out, through any of a number of dysfunctions that plague families. The wounded adult child has had few plateaus in life when life felt peaceful, joyous. The spirit of the adult child has been wounded, leaving the individual unable to be the whole person God meant him or her to be.

The faith community, in its ideal, presents a powerful arena of healing for the adult recovering from damage of the past: the community embraces values of redemption from exile, resurrection from loss, and unconditional love. Yet the faith community, in its reality, can also appear to be an unwelcoming fortress to an adult victim-survivor who holds anger and shame and who perhaps needs to break the silence about injustice or abuse from the past: the covenant community embraces values of peacefulness and meekness, of forgiving seven times, or even seventy times seven.

How does the community of faith live up to its ideal in nurturing and guiding the healing process of the adult victim-survivor? In particular, how does the pastoral caregiver, clergy or lay, become an agent of restoration for the adult in recovery from childhood brokenness?

The task of "care of the soul" has been a function of clergy and lay ministers for centuries, grounded on the belief that the soul needs to be tended to and nurtured just as the body does. God intends individuals to lead lives of wholeness, joy, and love. Because the church is guided by God's will of wholeness, the task of care of the soul is integral in the work of the church.

The caregiver for the soul can foster healing when a person's relationship with God has been infected by anger at God, by a sense of being abandoned by or punished by God, by a sense of being unworthy before God, or by a fear of God. The caregiver for the soul is able to help the broken individual redeem her hope, restore his inner joy, renew her trust, and reconcile with his community.

A CASE STUDY

Cindy, a young college student away from home, was reluctant to take part in the activities of her campus ministry. She attended worship periodically but resisted becoming a part of any nonworship activities of her church. A friend persuaded her to set up an appointment with the campus minister, Reverend Paul.

In their meeting, Cindy confided to Reverend Paul that she had been touched inappropriately by a church school teacher as a preteen. She had been unable to talk with her parents about it but often pleaded with her parents not to make her go to church school anymore. Her parents insisted that she continue with church school until her confirmation at fifteen. Her experience in church school for those several years was one of hypervigilance, fear, and shame.

Cindy told Reverend Paul that she was afraid to get involved with the campus ministry because she still felt ashamed about what had happened. Reverend Paul pressed Cindy for more details and learned that her experience with the church school teacher had occurred several times during one summer, when the church school class took picnics to a local lake. Reverend Paul believed that Cindy had probably misinterpreted the contact by the teacher. He explained to Cindy that, in her preadolescent confusion, she might have blown meaningless touches out of proportion. She had nothing to be ashamed of, he assured her, because in all probability nothing had happened. Cindy eventually fell away from the campus church altogether.

Several years later, Cindy graduated from college and settled down in a small town, beginning a career as an elementary school teacher. She began attending a local church and eventually found herself in the pastor's study to talk. She again confided the incidents in her hometown church, this time adding what the campus minister had said. Cindy shared that she still felt ashamed and confused about it all. The pastor, Reverend Baker, listened and offered to Cindy the opportunity to talk more about what she had been through.

After several meetings together, Cindy opened up to Reverend Baker that her older brother had also molested her during her preteen years. Reverend Baker suggested to Cindy some resources to read about childhood sexual abuse and gave her a referral to a local mental health professional. Cindy eventually joined a therapy group with other women survivors of childhood abuse. She continued to turn to Reverend Baker periodically with questions about forgiveness and about why God had allowed her abuse to happen. Cindy's involvement and investment in the life of the church increased as she felt more trust and healing.

Reverend Paul and Reverend Baker both offered Cindy a caring and pastoral ear, sincerely wanting to help this young woman with her shame. Reverend Paul, however, missed an opening for healing, whereas Reverend Baker traveled with Cindy an important step beyond caring and empathy, and ultimately served as an integral part of Cindy's recovery.

THE PERVASIVENESS OF DYSFUNCTION

Statistics on alcoholism, mental illness, child sexual abuse, and domestic violence are staggering. In recognizing the impact on families of any of these forms of trauma, it becomes clear that the number of children deeply affected by family dysfunction is high. Although some of these children receive help for integrating the trauma while they are still young, others learn to defend against the pain through repression, denial, dissociation, or acting out. Many enter adulthood as wounded as when they were first affected. Considering the pervasiveness of family dysfunction, the number of adults carrying a heavy load of unresolved childhood pain could be epidemic.

Many individuals in pain turn first to the church or the temple for counsel, whether it be from a clergyperson, a religious educator, or a respected lay member. According to a 1992 Gallup poll, as reported in an American Association of Pastoral Counselors petition, 66 percent of respondents preferred to turn for help to a professional who represents spiritual values and beliefs. In addition, 81 percent preferred to have their own values and beliefs integrated into the helping process.[2]

What an indictment it is on our churches when this resource proves to be inadequate for one suffering from long-neglected emotional or spiritual wounding. On the other hand, what a testimony it is to the power of the church when pastoral caregivers do effectively minister to the wounds of adult survivors.

THE ORGANIZATION OF THIS BOOK

This book addresses the challenges of the pastoral caregiver in facilitating healing with individuals recovering from wounds of the past. Although ideally the pastoral caregiver is one among several caregivers in the healing process, he or she serves a unique pastoral function in the recovery.

The initial chapters of this book focus on identifying adult victim-survivors of childhood wounding, developing a profile of the adult in recovery from past abuse, and understanding the limitations of the pastoral caregiver as a resource in recovery. The middle chapters present an overview of the unique spiritual challenges of adult victim-survivors, including value conflicts, victim-survivor myths, and the role of forgiveness in healing. The later chapters address the significance of breaking the silence in recovery, the importance of confrontation, and the need to confront internal ghosts from the past. The final chapters point toward the redemptive healing process of letting go and moving on.

Each chapter offers case illustrations and vignettes of adult victim-survivors. These illustrations are derived from actual pastoral care encounters or from actual therapy processes. (Names and other identifying characteristics have been changed to ensure confidentiality and to protect the integrity of the pastoral office.)

Members of the population in question—adult survivors of childhood domestic trauma—are alternately identified throughout the book as survivors, victim-survivors, and adult children, as well as either parishioners or careseekers. It should be noted that this work addresses pastoral care with survivors not of catastrophic trauma but of domestic trauma. Although some of the theory may well apply to working with survivors of catastrophic trauma (for example, children of war, children of poverty, or children who have been victims of natural disasters), the intent of this book is to address the population of adult survivors of domestic trauma.

Each chapter of this book also outlines methods and skills useful to the pastoral careperson in working with the individual in recovery, and provides directed exercises that the caregiver can use to promote healing. An appendix offers sample guided meditations for use in pastoral care sessions.

This book is intended primarily for pastoral caregivers, both lay and clergy, who want to learn more about working with adult children in recovery. The tenor of the book will be particularly useful for the caregiver in guiding the adult child into increased communion with the spiritual dimensions of his or her recovery.

chapter one

Identifying Victim-Survivors

> We don't like the way we look. We think we're stupid, incompetent, untalented, and, in many cases, unlovable. We think our thoughts are wrong and inappropriate. We think our feelings are wrong and inappropriate. We believe we're not important.... We think we're inferior to and different than the rest of the world—not unique, but oddly and inappropriately different. We have never come to grips with ourselves.
> —Melody Beattie, *Codependent No More*

The feelings, thinking, relational dynamics, and spiritual life of the survivor of childhood wounding have all been affected by the suffering of the child. Yet, given the shame inherent in the wounding, added to the culture of the dysfunctional family that teaches its members to deny the pathology and to repress the pain, survivors work hard to conceal their pain from others, and they rarely broadcast their childhood history. The sanctity of the trusted pastoral relationship provides an exception.

As an aid to the caregiver in understanding and working with the victim-survivor, this chapter lays groundwork for identifying the population in need within the parish and draws a profile of the victim-survivor, with material integrated from adult child literature, sexual and physical abuse literature, and other resources.

THEORY AND BACKGROUND

David, in his mid-thirties, came into the pastor's study struggling with career questions: he faced the possibility of losing his current job, which was his second placement in a second career. David couldn't understand his dissatisfaction with his career choices. He was concerned about how another job change might affect his family, a wife and two young daughters. He also expressed worry about his mental health, wondering what was wrong with him in that he hadn't been satisfied with any of his jobs. David's wife had also voiced concern to him about his depression.

An exploration of his job history showed that David had not been unsuccessful in his chosen careers. He had done well and had been able to provide for his family, yet he felt a vague, nonspecific unhappiness. He felt little sense of direction regarding where his next career move might be. David also hinted at some difficulties in the marriage stemming from his passivity and lack of direction.

In sharing his family history, David revealed that he had grown up with a mother who was manic-depressive and had attempted suicide several times during his teenage years. David, being the oldest child, felt a responsibility to keep his mother stable, to keep her alive, and to keep his family together during the chronic state of crisis. Neither his father nor his mother talked with the children about his mother's condition. Yet David saw his mother's visible unhappiness: he worried through the days his mother spent lying on the couch, he listened to her uncontrollable weeping, and he feared losing her. David's adolescent life revolved around home as he gave up extracurricular activities, cut down on his social and dating life, and tried to tend to his mother's emotional and mental needs.

David wondered in the pastor's office whether his home environment during his teenage years had filtered into his adulthood, affecting his enjoyment of life. He wondered whether his guilt about his career unhappiness and his lack of assertiveness in the marriage were related to his family history.

Identifying the Population

The linking of the past with the present is a common thread among adult victim-survivors of childhood wounding: unhealed wounds and/or unfinished business from the past fester in current life struggles as a challenge for healing. David himself made the connection that his career dissatisfaction might be rooted in childhood trauma. His questioning his own mental health in the face of no evidence that his mental health was in jeopardy also provided a clue that his current crisis had roots in his past.

How does the pastoral caregiver identify the population of adults who are hurting from childhood wounding? What clues hint to the pastor that the issues a parishioner brings to the pastoral relationship may run deeper than a struggle with current day-to-day problems? The pastoral caregiver who hears disclosure of the unhealed past from parishioners is receiving a summons to join in the challenge of healing.

The Dysfunctional Family

The population addressed includes adults who grew up in homes where parents or guardians were physically or emotionally unavailable to care for the needs of the children. These homes include a range of settings: alcoholic homes, homes where physical or sexual abuse occurred, homes in which a parent or a sibling suffered from a chronic physical or mental illness, and overly religious homes in which rigid and inflexible moral standards were set for the family members.

These environments tend to set up common conflicts, including the conflict of the family facade versus the family culture behind closed doors, and the conflicting needs of underattended children and overstressed adults. Children growing up in these environments are candidates for developing a predictable set of defenses in reaction to these conflicts, such as repression of feeling, denial of the extent of the family problems, and chronic low-grade depression and guilt.

Who do these children become as adults? Identifiable sets of characteristics and qualities include a certain seriousness, a lack of spontaneity, and a sense of overresponsibility. The person might operate with a quickness to try to take care of the feelings of others while not actively caring for his or her own needs. He does not take time for himself; she does not stand up for herself. Often the adult survivor displays a tendency to avoid conflict or a difficulty tolerating unavoidable conflict. These and a host of other characteristics tend to characterize the population of adult children.

Janet Woititz, in her work on adult children of alcoholic families, has developed a profile that is transferable to adults from other dysfunctional childhood backgrounds.[1] Codependent literature also offers profiles that can be helpful in understanding and identifying adult children. Although initially coined to describe the relationship of a spouse to an alcoholic, the term "codependency" has come to be used to describe a range of unhealthy relationships. As a defining word for the population of adult survivors of childhood wounding, "codependency" refers to the tendency to develop relationships based on caretaking, control, submerging of one's separate identity, and dependency on the dysfunction of another to feel needed. Melody Beattie offers a useful list of questions regarding codependency and adult children.[2]

For the pastoral caregiver, a familiarity with the themes of codependency and adult children is useful for identifying those who struggle with the legacy of a dysfunctional background and for helping these persons find a peace with their pasts and with themselves.

Post-Traumatic Stress Disorder

Some adult children, as a result of prolonged childhood trauma, suffer from the clinical syndrome Post-Traumatic Stress Disorder (delayed onset), or PTSD. PTSD often afflicts individuals who have histories of childhood abuse or other early traumatic experiences and who continue to feel haunted by the past, especially when confronted with life events that remind them of the earlier trauma.

These individuals tend to develop difficulties with intensity of feeling, self-destructive behavior or behavior harmful to others, struggles with trust and closeness, self-medication through alcohol or other drugs, and dissociative problems, among other issues. (Dissociation is a defense that entails separation of oneself from one's experience.) The *Diagnostic Criteria from DSM-IV* (309.81) provides a list of identifying symptoms of individuals suffering from PTSD.[3]

The Spiritual Profile

The parishioner suffering from unhealed childhood wounds also tends to develop an identifiable "spiritual profile." The spiritual life tends to be weighted heavily with guilt and unrealistic expectations of self. A spiritual perfectionism leaves little room for grace. More often than not, God is experienced as critical and judgmental. Although the individual might embrace the concept of unconditional love as something God feels toward others, she or he has difficulty accepting that God might have unconditional love toward her or him. The individual feels unworthy and undeserving of grace. (Chapters 3 and 4 address more fully the spiritual life of the adult child.)

A questionnaire that focuses on the spiritual life of the adult child follows:

An Inner Life Checklist

	Always	Frequently	Sometimes	Never
1. Do you feel hopeful about the future?	4	3	2	1
2. Do you feel close to the important people in your life?	4	3	2	1
3. Do you feel able to trust others?	4	3	2	1
4. Do you feel "numb"?	1	2	3	4
5. Do you feel shame?	1	2	3	4
6. Do you feel God cares about you?	4	3	2	1
7. Do you feel close to God?	4	3	2	1

8. Do you feel judged by God?	1	2	3	4
9. Do you feel God is punishing you?	1	2	3	4
10. Do you experience moments of joy?	4	3	2	1
11. Do you feel "at peace"?	4	3	2	1
12. Do you feel low self-worth?	1	2	3	4

This questionnaire points to how the spirit of the person (his or her intelligence, affective life, self-consciousness, capacity to relate to others, and sense of freedom and responsibility) has been wounded, oppressed, or broken by the trauma of the past. A higher score indicates an open, dynamic spiritual life, whereas a lower score suggests a spirit that is blocked or hurting. Further inquiry would address the extent to which the pain from the past is affecting the ability of the person to live a full, gratifying, enjoyable life in the present—to live as the whole person God created her or him to be.

METHOD

Quite a few members of the average community fit these profiles, and many of these have come out of a background of some sort of trauma or dysfunction. An understanding and awareness of these characteristics can be useful to the caregiver when a parishioner presents for pastoral care issues that seem rooted in a traumatic childhood background. This knowledge provides a road map to explore the historical person, questioning what might be festering from childhood, offering guidance in psychoeducation, and inviting further healing.

The Invitation to Self-Disclosure

Often self-disclosure of childhood wounding is veiled and indirect. Simple, nonintrusive questions can help elicit a disclosure about childhood trauma or childhood wounding when the parishioner is ready to share. Ministers, rabbis, or priests can develop a repertoire of questions to ask when they sense that unhealed wounding or unfinished childhood business is negatively affecting a careseeker's current life experience. Ideally, the questions allow the pastoral caregiver to move into painful historical material in a way that is not invasive for the careseeker.

Simple, succinct questions help avoid confusion. Inquiries might range from "How old do you feel right now?" "Does she remind you of anyone from your past?" "Have you experienced this kind of loss before?" or "Are these feelings familiar?" to the more direct "Did anyone in your family have a drinking problem when you were growing up?" or "Were you ever abused as a child?" An intuited sense of how safe the careseeker is currently feeling, as well as the comfort level of the caregiver in inviting a deeper level of self-disclosure, is an important barometer of when to ask further questions and how direct to be in the inquiry.

Psychoeducation

In the initial stages of the pastoral care process, the carer can offer literature on adult children of dysfunctional families or survivors of childhood abuse, give the parishioner a profile or checklist to consider, or even suggest a twelve-step group for the parishioner to attend (for example, an ALANON adult child group) in order to get a sense of whether and/or how the group applies to him or her. Psychoeducation about the developmental and spiritual issues of adult children provides a platform for beginning conscious healing.

David, the young father presented at the beginning of this chapter, was given several articles on adult children of dysfunctional families. After reading the literature, he returned to the office expressing excitement, having identified strongly with the material. Through his identification with the stories of others who had experienced similar struggles, he reported feeling already less alone and more hopeful.

Eventually, David was referred to a group for adult children. Through his work in the group, David experienced increased self-respect, found the security within himself to engage in a thorough career assessment, and eventually entered a new career, which he found more fulfilling.

CONCLUSION

Grace is key for the pastoral caregiver in working with victim-survivors. It is important for the pastoral caregiver to take an approach using much affirmation, patience, and invitation, and little confrontation, pressure, or aggressiveness as to the need to resolve this pain.

The defense mechanisms the individual has developed have been functional, helping the person to survive experiences that have bordered on being unbearable. The depth of the wounding is not evident at the beginning of the process, and the extent of the pain involved in uncovering, cleansing, medicating, and binding the wounds varies from individual to individual.

The pastoral caregiver's approach would ideally be reflective of the unconditional, understanding, and empowering love of God. The pastor's manner needs to communicate a hope in the divine power to free, redeem, and renew the victim-survivor's life.

Although the caregiver can offer invitation and guidance, the healing process needs to be at the initiative and timing of the parishioner. Only she knows when she is ready. Only he knows how much he can bear. It takes courage and strength to step off the road and cut a new path.

chapter two

The Caregiver's Role

> Maybe, at a certain moment, it's best to think differently about the people we see. Maybe we shouldn't be emphasizing so strongly what "problems" they have, but how they get through their lives.
> —Robert Coles, *The Spiritual Life of Children*

The role of the pastor in the adult child's healing is different from the role of other resources in the recovery process. The pastor "thinks differently" about the people she or he sees, viewing the person from the perspective of one trained in theology, biblical studies, and pastoral care, as well as in the psychological disciplines. Spiritual growth is confidently expected, through God's grace, with the pastor serving as a potential mediator of redemptive power.

Ideally, the pastor serves the whole person, with a deep concern for the spirit of the individual, that vital and animated force of the person which includes intelligence, feeling, relatedness to others, self-consciousness, freedom, and responsibility. For the pastoral caregiver, the spiritual, emotional, and physical lives of the individual are intertwined and interdependent. The individual seeking care is a child of God, not merely a patient, a diagnosis, or a case study.

THEORY AND BACKGROUND

The multifaceted pastoral care role is often pivotal in healing, providing a service different from the professional psychotherapist, the self-help group, the twelve-step program, or other venues of victim-survivor healing. Whether in dealing with shame, forgiveness, experience of grace, or other spiritual concerns, or whether in resolving and integrating events of the past without overtly addressing the spiritual, the pastoral caregiver represents the presence of God in the healing process.

One young woman, who had grown up in a home with an alcoholic father, became engaged in a long-term psychotherapeutic relationship to sort through the legacy of this history. She periodically turned to her pastor with questions concerning her anger at God, her struggle with forgiveness of her parents, and her confused feelings about how God viewed her (having projected onto God the "father image" from her childhood). With her pastor, she was able to integrate her therapeutic learning in her spiritual development.

A Multifaceted Role

Several images and metaphors are helpful in understanding the role of the pastoral caregiver in the victim-survivor's healing. The pastor, in working with the survivor of childhood wounding, functions as a spiritual guide, a teacher, a companion, a midwife, a witness, and a mediator of divine grace.

Spiritual Guide. The pastoral caregiver is a spiritual guide, one who encourages the spiritual life of the individual, offering a faith perspective on the individual's healing. The pastor can interpret the recovery process through the lenses of grace, of resurrection, of exile and the promised land, and of forgiveness. The pastor offers prayer as a hope for healing, reframing the wounding in the language of prayer. The pastor addresses the spirit of the individual.

Robert Coles remembers from his training as a pediatric resident in child psychiatry the language used to describe the children he worked with:

> One boy had "serious problems"; another boy was in "serious trouble"; a girl required "prolonged treatment," while the next girl

had, we all knew, "major emotional difficulties." On the other hand, a supervisor would remind us, rather rarely, it seemed, that some people are "basically intact, psychologically," and even appear to be not only "sane" but of "solid psychological make-up."[1]

Coles wrote with gratitude of post-residency mentor Marion Putnam, who led him to a different way of looking at children: "Maybe we shouldn't be emphasizing so strongly what 'problems' they have, but how they get through their lives. Since we've all got our problems, it's what we do with them that distinguishes us."[2] Putnam offered a handle on the spiritual life of young patients.

The pastoral caregiver, as spiritual guide, sees the individual through a lens of wholeness more than through a lens of pathology. The individual is not so much a set of problems to be fixed, as a child of God on a pilgrimage.

Teacher. The pastor is also a teacher in the classroom of recovery. Sometimes this takes the shape of psychoeducation with the caregiver offering knowledge about recovery, such as the impact of trauma on children and adults, the effects of parental alcoholism or mental illness on children, and resources in the community for resolution of childhood wounding.

The teaching also takes the shape of reframing and challenging a parishioner's beliefs and worldview. A parishioner who believes she shouldn't get angry can be reminded of the anger of the prophets or the anger of Jesus at various points in the gospel accounts. The parishioner who finds it difficult to believe God cares about her; the parishioner who believes God is punishing her for acting out as a teenager; or the parishioner who wonders why he still feels hatred toward his father, believing that he forgave his father long ago—all present an opportunity for the caregiver to challenge theology and to offer different understandings.

Companion. The pastoral caregiver is also a companion, one who shares the journey for a time with the other seeker. The distinction of "being" versus "doing" is a helpful distinction here. The pastor as companion is called not to do the work for the pilgrim but to travel beside the pilgrim offering that potent message, "You are not alone."

When Jasmine reached "a light at the end of the tunnel" following a long, painful struggle to heal from the effects of sexual abuse as a young girl, she reflected on the times in her journey when she didn't think she could make it, didn't want to live anymore, and came close to taking her own life. She said that what kept her going was knowing that her pastor was there to call, to talk to, to go the distance with her.

Midwife. The metaphor of the midwife is also apt in understanding the pastoral caregiver's function. The work and pain of labor belong to the careseeker, whereas the caregiver adds guidance, coaching, encouragement, aid, assurance, and a measure of safety.

"I don't know if I can talk about this," "I don't know if I'm able to do this," and "Will this ever end?" are common refrains of the survivor in recovery. The pastor as midwife adds perspective by affirming the life-bearing quality of the pain.

Witness. The pastor also functions as a witness while individuals relive traumatic events that have not previously been shared with another. The individual is no longer alone with the memories. In witnessing, the pastor offers validity and credibility to a pain that has most often been minimized or discounted by the individual.

John, a successful father of three in his forties, relived in the pastor's office the terror of a fire that destroyed the family home when he was seven years old. He and his brother were trapped in an upstairs hallway until rescued by his mother, who, against the pleas of neighbors, had raced back into the burning house in a panic after realizing that two of her children were still inside. John recalled the incident as if it had just happened: he vividly remembered black smoke, his stinging lungs, and a sense of terror.

When he finished sharing his memory, John, his face pale and eyes filled with tears, looked desperately into his pastor's face and asked, "Did that really happen?" He needed validation, confirmation of his suffering. Having been witness to the reliving of John's trauma, the pastor replied, "Yes, it did." John sat in silence for a long time, until finally speaking the words "Thank you."

Mediator of Divine Grace. In the clergy role, the pastoral carer further functions as a mediator of divine grace. The survivor often looks to the counselor for moral judgment or acceptance, projecting onto the caregiver his or her own beliefs or fears about how God sees him or her. In this transference, the pastor becomes a representation of God's relationship toward the careseeker. As such, the acceptance, positive regard, and hope of the caregiver for the parishioner are a gift that runs deeper than the interpersonal level.

Reverend Danielson led a series of classes on elements of worship. Following a session on prayer of confession and assurance of pardon, Marie entered the pastor's study and talked about a longstanding feeling she had of something being existentially wrong with her, a chronic shame she had felt since childhood. She confided to Reverend Danielson a history of verbal abuse by an alcoholic mother and a feeling that somehow she was responsible for her mother's addiction. She asked Reverend Danielson, "Are we really forgiven?" Without hesitation, the pastor replied, "Yes, we are forgiven!" Marie wept in a catharsis of emotion that had been bottled inside for years. In a later discussion, she would refer to the hearing of those words—"Yes, we are forgiven"—as a gift of grace.

Pastoral Boundaries

Having identified some dimensions of the role of pastoral care in the healing of adult survivors of childhood wounding, it is critical to note also the limitations of the role. The importance of the issue of boundaries in working with adult children cannot be overestimated. The caregiver needs to understand and have confidence in the boundaries of his or her role, for the protection of the parishioner as well as for the protection of himself or herself. Carrie Doehring's work on relational boundaries in pastoral care and counseling addresses these concerns in depth.[3]

Although practitioners in most of the professional disciplines adhere to written standards of professional ethics, many faith groups are only now developing standards of professional ethics for their clergy. Those who provide pastoral care for survivors of childhood trauma need to familiarize themselves with professional ethics policies of their faith groups and might also benefit from reading the standards of professional ethics in other disciplines. An example of professional standards of ethics, from the American Association of Pastoral Counselors' "Code of Ethics," follows.

> We recognize the trust placed in and unique power of the therapeutic relationship. While acknowledging the complexity of some pastoral relationships, we avoid exploiting the trust and dependency of clients. We avoid those dual relationships with clients (e.g., business or close personal relationships) which could impair our professional judgment, compromise the integrity of the treatment, and/or use the relationship for our own gain.[4]

The Range of Recovery Resources

The pastoral care role in the recovery process of adult survivors of childhood wounding is ideally an adjunct role, with the ministry being a piece of a larger recovery quilt. The question of when to refer is a question recognizing the limits of pastoral care. The clergyperson who does not easily refer to other helping professionals risks losing energy for doing healing work and may become burned out, cynical, or hopeless about being able to effect change. The clergyperson who does not easily refer also risks doing more harm than good for the survivor.

In an adjunct role, the pastoral caregiver recognizes the overwhelming nature of the work for many survivors, is aware of the depth of pain in the healing of childhood wounds, and is prepared to lead the parishioner to other avenues of healing as the need becomes evident.

Denise entered her pastor's office to talk about the difficulty that the church's new inclusive language policy presented for her. Denise said she didn't want to think about God as father or mother, because either brought up negative associations. Denise tearfully and hesitatingly confided a history of sexual abuse by her father with covert permission by her mother.

Pastor Kent gave Denise a referral to a group for survivors of child sexual abuse. The group gave Denise a place to work through the psychological and emotional impact of her abuse, whereas in Kent's office she was able to talk about her developing image of God and the healing of her relationship with God, an added gift of her recovery work.

The caregiver needs to become familiar with the resources in his or her community, including mental health providers who specialize in doing trauma work, and psychiatrists who are skilled in survivor work and are available for medical evaluations. Although resources vary from community to community, options for referral may also include twelve-step groups, psychoeducational groups, trauma-focused groups, individual psychotherapy, and psychiatric services.

Gender Issues in Referral

Often an abuse survivor is reluctant to trust a caregiver of the same gender as the perpetrator of the abuse. For example, a female abuse survivor might have difficulty trusting a male caregiver if the childhood abuse was suffered at the hands of a male caretaker. The pastor needs to be respectful of this dynamic and to help the survivor find caregivers of the gender which feels most safe for the survivor.

METHOD

Working with other professionals, referring the careseeker to mental health specialists, and helping the careseeker develop a strong recovery and support network require several basic techniques on the part of the pastoral caregiver.

Developing a Referral List

The first basic technique involves developing or obtaining a list of resources in the community, including female and male professionals who specialize in working with trauma survivors; professionals who run psychodynamic therapy groups; agencies or institutions offering psychoeducational groups; twelve-step meetings; and psychiatrists of both genders. Second, the pastoral caregiver needs to know what groups are appropriate for specific referral, and when to refer for individual psychotherapy.

Psychoeducational groups are helpful in initial stages of healing, as the adult child begins to understand the dynamics and the process. Twelve-step groups are helpful for support and guidance from peers. Self-help groups are particularly useful for individuals with limited financial resources who do not have insurance coverage for professional help. Psychotherapy groups are helpful to those who feel the need for professional leadership and input in an ongoing group, or for those who may feel overwhelmed by the emotions and ramifications of the healing process.

Individual psychotherapy is also an important referral when a parishioner is feeling overwhelmed by the process. Particularly in cases of a history of prolonged or severe childhood trauma, when repressed memories have started to surface, or when symptoms are intruding on relationships or on routine functioning, referral to a professional specialist is necessary.

Establishing a Self-Help Group

In areas where twelve-step meetings have not been established, the pastor can consider starting a meeting in the church. Central headquarters for twelve-step programs can provide information on setting up a regularly scheduled meeting.

For further information on starting an adult child group, the pastoral caregiver can receive information from this address:

ALANON Family Group Headquarters
1372 Broadway, Seventh Floor
New York, New York 10018-0862
(phone) 212-302-7240

Information about starting an Incest Survivors Anonymous group can be obtained from this address:

Incest Survivors Anonymous
P.O. Box 17245
Long Beach, California 90807-7245
(phone) 310-428-5599

Beth Ann shared with her pastor a history of growing up in a home with an alcoholic father. Although she was already in a long-term psychotherapeutic relationship to work through the psychodynamic end of her dysfunctional history, Beth Ann felt the need for a support group to listen to and share her experience with others. Beth Ann and the pastor invited two other individuals to be a part of a committee to establish an ALANON Adult Child Group in the church, the first in the area. The initial meeting drew about a dozen attendees. After five years, the group customarily drew a crowd of fifty. Beth Ann found immeasurable support from the other members of the group.

Obtaining Informed Consent

Although it can be important for the pastoral caregiver to talk freely with other professionals who are providing care to the parishioner, the confidentiality of the pastoral relationship needs also to be respected. Discussion with other professionals should not occur without the consent of the parishioner. The pastoral caregiver should candidly let the parishioner know the reasons for wanting to speak with other professionals and should share the content of conversations with the parishioner. This will solidify the trust developing in the pastoral relationship.

An informed consent written for the parishioner's signature might be developed along these lines:

> I give _____ (caregiver's name) permission to communicate with _____ (professional's name) of _____ (name of counseling center or agency) concerning my clinical, medical, and/or pastoral care.
>
> _____ (parishioner's signature)
> _____ (caregiver's signature)
> _____ (date)

CONCLUSION

By nature, the wounds that the victim-survivor carries into adulthood hold spiritual ramifications. The pastoral dimension, integrated into a recovery process, opens the door for the process to be not just an emotional or mental recovery, or a resolution of unhealthy personality dynamics, but a healing of the whole person. As the pastoral caregiver is respectful of his or her limitations and of the necessary role of other resources in the journey toward wholeness, he or she is able most fully to be a mediator of redemptive power.

chapter three

Paradoxes of Value

> For the enemy has pursued me,
>   crushing my life to the ground,
>   making me sit in darkness like those long dead.
> Therefore my spirit faints within me;
>   my heart within me is appalled.
>
>   . . .
>
> I stretch out my hands to you;
>   my soul thirsts for you like a parched land.
>   —Psalm 143:3–4, 6

The imagery from the psalmist is apt for survivors of childhood domestic trauma. This is a population who as children were ignored, abused, or neglected by guardians, who were emotionally and developmentally stifled ("crushing my life to the ground"), who hid from parents in closets and under beds ("making me sit in darkness like those long dead"), and who experience both rage and denial about the deprivation of their childhood ("my heart within me is appalled"). These are also individuals who yearn for a response to that spiritual emptiness and who draw on a hope deep within ("my soul thirsts for you like a parched land").

Spiritual emptiness can be fertile soil for redeeming spirituality. Survivors of childhood domestic trauma who come for pastoral care are poised to make leaps in spiritual development. This chapter addresses one aspect of the restoration of the spirit of the trauma survivor, that of resolving common areas of spiritual conflict.

THEORY AND BACKGROUND

Merle Jordan uses the phrase "secular scripture" to describe those teachings, values, and beliefs which "operate in the human psyche as though they came down on tablets from Mount Sinai.... They are filled with shoulds, oughts, and musts.... These teachings appear as sacred, revealed truths, but in reality they are destructive lies."[1] Secular scripture also describes those church teachings which seem rooted in scripture yet function to oppress. Secularized scripture adapts, adjusts, and thereby distorts sacred scripture to fit the values and modes of thought of the secular culture. An overt example might be some churches' use of Paul's teaching "Wives, be subject to your husbands" (Eph. 5:22) to condone an imbalance of power in marriage relationships. Sarah said one day in counseling, "I don't like church. They give you all the 'pat answers.' And the pat answers may in fact be the answers, but it's a process, and they're not pat." Secularized scriptures boil down authentic scripture into pat answers.

Often in dysfunctional families, secular scriptures of the family, combined with those taught by the community of faith, perpetuate dysfunction. Several areas of spiritual conflict, grounded in secular scripture, generally arise for adult children involved in a healing or recovery process. These conflicts include selflessness versus selfhood (a conflict of serving others versus paying attention to one's own needs), meekness versus assertiveness (a conflict of submissiveness versus taking responsibility for oneself), and forgiveness versus self-affirmation (a conflict involving letting go of past wounding without ignoring the injustice). These conflicts are paradoxical conflicts, resolved not through battle, in which one value wins out over another, but through integration, in which several seemingly incongruent values are embraced mutually.

Selflessness

The first and major spiritual paradox challenging adult children stems from biblical injunctions about selflessness, exhorted in such gospel passages as "No one has greater love than this, to lay down one's life for one's friends" (John 15:13) and "So the last will be first and the first will be last" (Matt. 20:16). A parallel paradigm in the Hebrew Scriptures can be found in such passages as the story of Ruth:

> Where you go, I will go;
>   where you lodge, I will lodge;
> your people shall be my people,
>   and your God my God. (1:16)

The scriptural mandate of serving others comes fairly easily for the adult child, who has learned to lose his or her own wounded self in the role of servanthood in a dysfunctional family system. Adult children are typically caretakers, putting their own needs second to the needs of those around them, tending to the feelings of significant (and not-so-significant) others to the neglect of tending to their own feelings. This kind of service, however, far from being spiritually rewarding, is spirit-depleting for the wounded adult child. Serving others becomes a codependency, with little sense of self separate from the role of service.

The secular scripture of the dysfunctional family draws on the biblical principle of servanthood to designate selfishness as a grave sin. Independence or differentiation in turn gets labeled as selfishness (see chapter 6). Adult children typically feel "selfish" when they begin to work on recovery from wounds of the past. Somehow, to spend time on oneself betrays the value of serving others; to give voice to one's own feelings betrays the family.

After Anita's mother divorced her father (an alcoholic and addictive gambler), ten-year-old Anita became a sounding board for her mother's loneliness, financial struggles, and constant weariness. Anita cleaned house and cooked, watched after her younger brothers while her mother worked a night job, and in general became a surrogate spouse for her hurting mother. Anita's weekend visits with her father were filled with attending AA meetings with him, listening to his inventory of wrongs, and, in time, entertaining her new stepsister while her father attended her brothers' sporting events.

Anita was the model child, praised to others by both parents for being so mature and helpful. Yet Anita felt lost in the midst of it all. When as an adult Anita began to work on her feelings in counseling, she continually voiced a conviction that she was being "selfish" talking about her experience.

To tend to self, for adult children, feels like a betrayal of those they love; to care for the self is dissonant with behavior learned in and followed since childhood. Paul, in his letter to the Galatians, pairs freedom and service: "For you were called to freedom; only do not use your freedom as an opportunity for the flesh, but through love be servants of one another" (5:13). The spiritual challenge for the adult child is to develop a differentiated sense of self, a sense of freedom that serves others out of conscious choice rather than out of unconscious need to maintain an identity (which often results in resentment). The spiritual challenge is to maintain the gift of ease in the serving position—the caretaking gift—while also developing a sense of self-worth that values caring for oneself. In a functional system, the ability to care for self is integral to healthy giving within the system.

Meekness

"Blessed are the meek" (Matt. 5:5), the first of the Beatitudes, shapes another paradox challenging adult children. The sanctity of meekness and humility in the Gospels finds its parallel in the image of the suffering servant in Isaiah:

> He was oppressed and he was afflicted,
>   yet he did not open his mouth;
> like a lamb that is led to the slaughter,
>   and like a sheep that before its shearers is silent,
>   so he did not open his mouth. (53:7)

In secularized scripture, the suffering servant image becomes translated into a value of submissiveness and passivity. Survivors of childhood trauma typically have learned that their feelings and needs are unimportant. "Don't talk, don't trust, and don't feel," unspoken rules for children in dysfunctional families as identified by Claudia Black,[2] make for a meek spirit, in the secular understanding of meek as submissive and passive. The secular injunction against passionate feelings of anger, pain, outrage, and even intense joy or love paves the way, for the adult child, for a restricted range of affect blunted by shame, low self-esteem, diminished self-worth, or low-grade depression.

The unspoken secular scriptures of the dysfunctional family—don't talk, don't trust, and don't feel—are girded by the secularized scriptures taught in many churches and synagogues, scriptures such as "Don't ever hurt another person's feelings" (which might happen if you assert yourself), "Good people don't get angry," and "It's best to suffer in silence." The nonauthentic, passive self is reinforced and validated through a misguided understanding of Judeo-Christian teachings of the suffering servant and of the "turn-the-other-cheek" model from Luke: "Bless those who curse you, pray for those who abuse you. If anyone strikes you on the cheek, offer the other also; and from anyone who takes away your coat do not withhold even your shirt" (6:28–29).

"There was never any room for my feelings when I was a child," Anita said, "because my parents were suffering so much. It was like their pain was the only pain that mattered. After all, I was a child. I wasn't as important as them. I felt guilty if I got angry at them or if I needed something from them. I didn't want to burden them any more than they already felt." As a child, Anita's feelings were restricted to her bedroom, where behind closed doors she would spend hours crying alone. As an adult, Anita felt frozen inside, numb. Whenever she was asked how she was feeling, Anita would have to respond, "I don't know."

The spiritual challenge for the adult child is to acknowledge and affirm a wide repertoire of authentic feelings, including anger, pain, joy, and love, gaining freedom from the spirit-deadening legacy of having been controlled by inadequate caretakers. The spiritual challenge is also an assertiveness of self that does not devalue or dominate the self of another.

In actuality, the suffering servant of the Hebrew Scriptures is neither weak nor passive but, rather, is obedient to an acultural voice within that transcends abuse and deprivation, standing for redemption from brokenness. The meekness Jesus calls for is not submissiveness but an attitude of humility that does not claim control over or wrest power from others.

For the healthy spirit, neither dominance nor submissiveness is necessary, just as denial of feeling is unnecessary, in relating to others. One need not blame others nor shame oneself. The meek are those who are gentle and show patience yet who are able to talk, trust, and feel. The suffering servant is one who, rather than resigning herself or himself to oppression, transcends suffering and humiliation to usher in redemption.

Forgiveness

Marie Fortune writes of forgiveness,

> Most importantly, forgiveness happens in its own time and cannot be rushed from the outside. It may take one year or thirty. Pastors or counselors can be present to a victim as she/he struggles with a need and desire to forgive. They can do whatever they can to mediate justice in her/his experience. They can witness to God's presence and power. But they cannot force a victim to forgive.[3]

The issue of forgiveness is one of the most difficult challenges for the adult child who has felt hurt, abandoned, abused, or neglected by significant adults during childhood. Forgiveness has many different meanings and understandings, and it can sometimes feel like an added weight for the wounded adult struggling for healing of the spirit.

In the simple secular understanding of forgiveness, the offender apologizes and the wronged person accepts the apology. Consequently, the relationship is reconciled. The wronged person lets go of the feeling of having been hurt, excusing the other person from fault. Some clergy and rabbis even teach their parishioners that to forgive means to forget.

Forgiveness for adult children, in this understanding of the process, can result in an invalidation of the wounded child, an ignorance or denial of the pain resulting from the caretaker's harmful behavior. For many adult children, the pain has become a part of the self; when forgiveness means having to excuse the behavior or deny the pain, forgiveness devalues the self of the adult child.

Peter, who lived with memories of cruel domestic violence at the hands of his father, was asked if he felt anger toward his father. He said, "No. We [brothers, sisters, and mother] all forgave him a long time ago. I just need to get over it and not dwell on the past." It was months later, as Peter finally confronted his anger in pastoral counseling, when he passionately said, "I thought I forgave my father for what he did, but I don't think I ever realized how much my whole life was affected by his abuse. I don't know if I could ever really forgive him!"

Two points should be noted in developing a spiritual understanding of forgiveness for adult children of childhood domestic trauma. The first is that most often the offender does not come to the child with an apology or in an attitude of repentance. As often as not, the offender denies the abuse or minimizes the impact of the trauma on the child.

Second, the offense is one that involves the unequal relationship between adult and child. The child is dependent on the adult in a dynamic that Judeo-Christian ethics understands as a sacred trust. (In instances where the abuse occurred at the hands of an older sibling, cousin, or neighborhood child, the relationship is a violation of a different order, yet it is still an imbalance of power.)

Adult children don't need to forgive, in the secular understanding of the act. This type of forgiveness can stifle the healing process. The parishioner may need permission *not* to forgive (in the secular sense) in order to work through the anger and rage without pressure to "get on with it" and to "be a better person." Paradoxically, not forgiving gives the adult child the grace to work through the anger, leading an unforgiving spirit toward an internal forgiveness. For the adult child, forgiveness, rather than being a relational forgiveness (a reconciliation of broken trust), needs to be an internal spiritual process.

Wendy Maltz and Beverly Holman describe a forgiveness that is self-affirming: "It can allow and encourage the survivor to accept her own humanness, develop compassion toward herself, remove remaining self-blame, and release herself from constantly experiencing negative feelings toward old family members."[4] Jesus shows a unique style of forgiveness in his crucifixion: "Father, forgive them; for they do not know what they are doing" (Luke 23:34). Jesus' forgiveness turned the abuse and the wrong over to an ultimate authority. Jesus' forgiveness did not devalue his suffering or ignore the reality of the crucifixion. In a similar vein, Judeo-Christian teachings about justice neither devalue the suffering nor ignore the reality of the wrong. Rather, Judeo-Christian teachings place confidence in a higher order: "But let justice roll down like waters, and righteousness like an ever-flowing stream" (Amos 5:24).

Forgiveness, for the adult child, is a process and a continuum, rather than—as the secular scripture would teach—a one-time act that makes everything better. The process of forgiveness is a gradual one that works as internal redemption from suffering without necessarily making everything better.

For the adult child, spiritual forgiveness is different from a reconciliation process through which healing works two ways and a caring relationship is restored. Adult children in healing gradually let go of the myth of reconciliation and work toward a restoration of self rather than toward a restoration of relationship. Restoration of self comes through naming the wrong, giving voice to the pain, and moving away from the false claim the wrong makes on the spirit. With this restoration comes a gradual transforming of the claim that the suffering makes on the spirit.

METHOD

Healing from childhood wounding involves integration of these spiritual paradoxes, a deep theological struggle. Adult children of dysfunctional families, through their own experience of oppression, have a metaphorical finger on the pulse of Judeo-Christian teaching. The pastoral caregiver draws on that experience in working with the adult child toward healing.

In leading the parishioner to an integration of conflicting values, the caregiver can reframe distorted understandings of servanthood, meekness, and forgiveness, and challenge secular scriptures such as "Good people don't get angry," or "It's best to suffer in silence." The pastor can use biblical references when appropriate to support self-affirming values or to negate secular scriptures. This reframing and challenging is the sharing of a theology of grace.

Servanthood

Useful in a reframing of the servanthood model is dialogue with the careseeker about the difference between caregiving and enabling, the difference between taking-care-of and codependency. The pastor can ask the parishioner to cite examples of healthy versus unhealthy caregiving.

As a teenager, Courtney used to put her alcoholic mother to bed regularly. Her mother would drink until she passed out in a chair, whereupon Courtney would change her mother into a nightgown and struggle to get her into the bedroom and into bed. When Courtney left for college, her mother called her the day after she moved into her dorm room. Her mother said, "I must have gotten really drunk last night! Can you believe I passed out in the chair in the living room? That's where I woke up this morning!"

Courtney shared this story with her pastor as an example of how, trying to be helpful to her mother, she had actually enabled her mother's denial of the seriousness of her drinking problem. Courtney was beginning to realize the need for a new ethic of serving others.

As a balance to scriptural passages of servanthood, the pastor can draw on scriptural passages of freedom. Examples might include "Let the dead bury their own dead" (Luke 9:60) and the Exodus story. If the parishioner experiences some confusion with seemingly conflicting passages, he or she can be encouraged to use the conflict for reflection, journal writing, and further development of a spiritual understanding of servanthood. The parishioner needs to be challenged to address the importance of a sense of self apart from the caregiving role.

Following her divorce, Maxine said, "I don't know who I am anymore. All my life I've been taking care of other people. First I had to take care of the little ones when my father got disabled and my mother was 'going crazy.' When I got married I thought I would get some freedom from having to take care of other people, but then I found myself taking care of my husband, who couldn't do anything without me. Then when the twins came along I had to take care of them for eighteen years until they moved off to college. And I'm still having to take care of them. Susan called me the this morning to ask me how much towels cost!

"All my life I've been taking care of other people. I don't want to do it anymore. I don't even know who I am. I want to be able to take care of me for a change."

Maxine struggled with the concepts of servanthood, selfishness, and self-affirmation. She felt profoundly moved by a prayer by Laurie Simon,[5] which was printed in material from a retreat she had attended. She felt this as a spiritual call in her struggle to integrate servanthood with selfhood:

> We can feel it within ourselves, each of us, our creativity awaiting life. Its voice whispers to us, forming that vision which is so intimately our own, yet asks to be shared. The words that require a page, the forms of color begging a canvas, the motion that needs to be danced, or the pattern of sounds which may breathe only through a flute.
>
> Dear God, help us to recognize these voices in ourselves; challenge us to realize them to life, in beauty; and help us to feel your presence in their whispers. Open us to your Word, and move us to answer your call among us. Amen.

Meekness

In the meekness versus assertiveness conflict, the pastoral caregiver needs initially to challenge the value of the survivor's submissiveness, and then to work with the survivor in developing a humble ego strength (an ability to maintain healthy ego functioning, particularly in times of stress or crisis). Challenging the passivity of the parishioner is the antithesis of the "Don't talk, don't trust, don't feel" model.

Talk. The pastor gives the survivor continuous permission and encouragement to talk about the trauma: "I'm glad you are talking about it now"; "Thank you for trusting me with that"; "I'm glad you could share that with me"; "You have a lot of courage to talk about all this." The pastoral care arena provides a setting where the parishioner can feel safe in talking about the childhood trauma, can feel accepted and not judged, and can begin to know the value of assertiveness.

Trust. A healthy, caring relationship with the pastor works toward healing a survivor's distrust of the world. The secular scripture "Don't trust" is challenged with each pastoral encounter, as the parishioner develops trust in the caregiver. The trust is reinforced through an unconditional positive regard by the caregiver for the parishioner, through honoring confidentiality and professional boundaries, and through genuinely joining the survivor in her or his healing.

Feel. The pastoral caregiver needs to mirror to the parishioner the feelings from childhood that the adult will not let himself or herself feel. The pastor continuously names feelings, communicating that it is all right to have anger, pain, fear, sadness, and so forth: "You must have been so angry"; "That little girl—*you*—must have really been hurting"; "I can't imagine going through that. It must have been so frightening"; "I can imagine how alone you must have felt as a child."

The parishioner can also be encouraged to keep a "feelings diary," routinely writing down at the end of the day each feeling experienced that day, for the duration of several weeks. Pastoral interpretation of the feelings diary will help the parishioner identify the spectrum of feelings he or she experiences. The caregiver should observe feelings that are notably absent from the chart: do the absent feelings represent feelings with which the parishioner is uncomfortable? The feelings diary can aid the survivor in awareness of his range of affect and can invite the survivor to expand on his or her repertoire of feelings.

Ego Strength. Having challenged the secular scripture teaching meekness as passivity, the pastor has the opportunity to work with the careseeker in developing a healthy ego strength from which the individual can respectfully say no, set limits, and assert herself or himself without cost to the personal power of the other. As the parishioner identifies situations in the past or present when her or his passivity did not serve well, the caregiver can use this as an opportunity for dialogue about boundaries and assertiveness.

Anita shared how she had several times taken her and her husband's ill dog to the veterinarian. Both working full-time jobs, she and her husband were both tired in the evenings. Each time the dog needed unexpected veterinary service, Anita's husband asked her to take the dog, saying he really needed the downtime. On returning from the vet, Anita would be confronted by her husband's anger when she told him how much the bill was. She silently resented him for not appreciating her doing the task and felt hurt by the anger he vented at her, but she felt little power to change anything.

In pastoral care, Anita identified the veterinary crises as incidents of passivity that served neither her nor her husband. Once when the dog needed emergency veterinary care, Anita asked her husband to take the dog in. When he returned and he told her how much the bill was, it was without anger. (He, not she, had written the check.) Anita felt empowered by this experience, not at the expense of her husband but only at the welcome cost of her submissive self, which she laid aside in asserting herself.

Forgiveness

Several interventions are useful in working with the survivor of childhood wounding to resolve the forgiveness paradox. The pastoral caregiver is in the unique position to empower the victim through the communication of God's grace in the pastoral care process.

Permission Not to Forgive. The pastoral caregiver can give the survivor permission not to forgive. From a clergyperson or rabbi, this permission carries tremendous weight and often feels like a gift to the survivor. The relief and freedom the careseeker feels from being let off the hook in this way can move her or him toward healing that paradoxically results in forgiveness.

Dialogue. For the pastor to share his or her own understandings of forgiveness and to raise challenging questions about the secular meanings of forgiveness prompts critical thinking and internal dialogue on the part of the pastoral careseeker. The careseeker can be encouraged to write journal entries or poetry about forgiveness as a means of putting the secular scripture on paper and beginning to recognize the holes in it. The caregiver can also represent an approach of justice in the dialogue, voicing the sure conviction that the careseeker has indeed been wronged, that no one—especially not a child—should have to go through the trauma and wounding that the victim experienced, and that the responsibility for the injustice lies with the offender.

A Forgiveness Questionnaire. The pastor can offer the parishioner a list of questions to address in reflection on the meaning of forgiveness, along the following lines:

1. How does the meaning of forgiveness change if there is no admitting of wrong or no apology from the other person?
2. What is the difference between a wrong done by one adult to another, and a wrong done by an adult to a child? Does forgiveness mean something different in each case?
3. Do you think of forgiveness as a one-time act or as a process that takes some time? Elaborate.
4. Some people believe that to forgive means to forget. Do you agree or disagree? Why or why not?
5. In Exodus, God says to Moses, "Whoever has sinned against me I will blot out of my book" (32:33). Jesus says that "whoever speaks against the Holy Spirit will not be forgiven" (Matt. 12:32). Do you believe there is unforgivable behavior?

6. Do you believe there should be conditions to forgiveness (such as apology, repentance, amends made, etc.)?

Scriptural Challenges. The pastoral caregiver can also have the wounded adult child read, reflect on, and write journal entries about scripture passages relating to forgiveness. These might include:

Exodus 32:33 (God says to Moses, "Whoever has sinned against me I will blot out of my book.")

Jeremiah 18:23 (Jeremiah asks of God, "Do not blot out their sin from your sight.")

Matthew 9:2-8 (the healing of the paralytic, with Jesus asking, "For which is easier, to say 'Your sins are forgiven,' or to say, 'Stand up and walk'?").

Luke 17:1-4 (including Jesus' words, "Be on your guard! If another disciple sins, you must rebuke the offender, and if there is repentance, you must forgive").

Matthew 12:32 (the sin "against the Holy Spirit").

CONCLUSION

However broken the adult child feels, however despairing, turning for help indicates hope. This hope needs to be reinforced and affirmed continually in pastoral care with adult children. The adult child has lived with a depleted reservoir of hope, depleted through betrayals and violations and broken promises, and through seeing things that no child (or adult, for that matter) should have to see. Yet the hope runs deep and the well seldom runs dry. Healing for the adult child involves reclaiming his or her hope as the agent in spiritual restoration. For the adult child, integration of the value paradoxes of selflessness versus selfhood, meekness versus assertiveness, and forgiveness versus self-affirmation is an important process in spiritual restoration.

chapter four

Myths of the Victim-Survivor

"I need something, I want something—I want to get off the hook!"

"For what?"

He begins to cry again. "For killing him, don't you know that? For letting him drown!"

"So, what is it you think you could have done to keep him from drowning?"

Tears flood his eyes again. He wipes them roughly away with his hand.

It is always this way. His mind shuts down. He cannot get by this burden, so overpowering that it is useless to look for a source, a beginning point. There is none.

"You don't understand," he says. "It has to be somebody's fault. Or what was the whole goddamn point of it?"

—Judith Guest, *Ordinary People*

The *Dictionary of Pastoral Care and Counseling* defines mythology as "the body of sacred tales that provide people with a vision of the cosmos and a set of ultimate values."[1] Adult children of dysfunctional families have developed powerful personal myths, both conscious and unconscious, as aids in their survival of childhood trauma. The personal myths of survivors help them hold on to a vision of a just and sensible world and to undergird ultimate values. The myths carry meaning and power that form some order out of chaos and keep the child from going crazy or from giving up the struggle for survival. The personal myths serve to impart dignity and humanity to experience that might otherwise be devoid of redeeming value.

Although personal myths of the victim-survivor are critical to the survival of the child, these myths are also impediments to the growth and development of the adult; they stifle the spirit of the adult. This chapter is about demythologizing, or letting go of the ideal of an external salvation separate from personal responsibility, and of replenishing the reservoir of energy that fuels internal health.

Anita struggled with moving beyond a myth of childhood as follows: "I just keep wishing my mother would love me the way I want her to. I keep thinking that if she would say she's sorry about what happened, and that she knows how hurt I've been by it all, then I could be happy. On the other hand, I know that's not the case. She might do all that, and I'd still be hurting and still have to work it through."

THEORY AND BACKGROUND

The common myths of the adult child include the myth that her unhealthy parents or family members are capable of caring, guiding, protective, and nurturing parenting (the myth of the good parent); the myth that if he is good enough, he can change the dysfunction of the family (the myth of control); the myth that someone out there will come one day to rescue her (the savior myth); the myth that everyone else lives a "normal" life and doesn't know the pain he knows (the myth of normalcy); and the myth that one day everything will be fine (the myth of restoration).

The Myth of the Good Parent

Young children hold on to an image of their parents as omniscient and all-powerful. Although this image fades as the child, with age, begins to develop a degree of independence and a sense of responsibility for self, even the older child tends to hold on to an image of his or her parents as powerful and as holders of answers to the important questions in life. The image of the parent as strong and knowledgeable aids a child in the development of a sense of safety in the world, a sense of security and well-being. A threat to this image, therefore, is a threat to the well-being of the child.

When a parent violates the trust of his or her role through physical assault, sexual abuse, broken alcoholic promises, or gambling fugues; when a parent is unable to meet the responsibilities of her or his role through prolonged lapses into depression or debilitating anxiety; when a parent falls grossly short of the ideal of omniscience and omnipotence, the child needs to defend her or his self against this threat to well-being. One important defense is denial of the inadequacy of the parent.

Jean's alcoholic father repeatedly left Jean, her mother, and her five younger brothers and sisters for alcoholic binges lasting months at a time. He would return with gifts for everyone in the family and verbal expressions of love, only to be gone again before the week was out. Jean loved her father and held him in high esteem throughout her childhood despite the continuous cycles of grief and disappointment. Jean truly believed her father was a good parent, notwithstanding evidence to the contrary.

The myth of the good parent, carried into adulthood, leaves the adult child in a position of continually setting herself or himself up for more hurt from inadequate parents, not recognizing the limitations of the parents. As an adult, Jean held on to her belief in what a good, loving parent her father was, yet she ached with each rejected phone call, each family gathering her father missed, each letter returned with no forwarding address. She drank heavily herself and was unable to develop a long-term intimate relationship with a partner. Until she found AA and began counseling, Jean held on to the myth that her father was a good parent.

The Myth of Control

Closely related to the myth of the good parent is the myth of control. When the parent is falling far short of the responsibilities of parenting, the child relies on denial as one defense and adds to the strength of the denial by blaming himself or herself for the trauma.

If the dysfunction cannot be my parent's fault, the child reasons, then it must be my fault.

During her elementary school years, Jean believed that if only she were good enough, her father would not leave anymore. When her father was home, she helped her mother keep the house spotless, she drew pictures for her father, she played intermediary when her parents fought. And each time her father left, she thought it was because she had done something wrong or had not done enough.

The myth of control is a belief the child holds that somehow she or he has the power to change the situation: to keep his parents from fighting, to keep her mother from getting depressed, to keep his father from drinking, to keep her uncle from exposing himself. This myth buttresses the myth of the good parent by, in the child's view, keeping the responsibility for domestic dysfunction with the child.

The myth of control, carried into adulthood, has implications for rigidity and lack of spontaneity. The adult child who operates out of the myth of control needs to do things right, to be responsible, and to follow a black-and-white script.

The Savior Myth

Many children in situations of domestic trauma develop a silent hope that they will be rescued, as fairy-tale characters are rescued. The child fantasizes a savior somewhere out there who knows her or his pain and aloneness. By this savior the child is loved, and with this savior the child belongs. The fantasy may be a vague hope in justice and authority, that "they" will come and help and that wrong will be righted. The fantasy may take the form of a silent question, such as "Why doesn't someone stop him (the perpetrator)?"

Judy was adopted as an infant into a family with an emotionally intrusive and verbally abusive mother. For years she held on to a fantasy that her "real" mother would come and get her.

For Joan, the myth took the shape of a vague rhetorical complaint: "Why don't 'they' do something about my parents' beating us?"

Peter loved the children's book *Are You My Mother?* in which a lost baby bird goes from one animal to another, to a boat, and to a crane asking the plaintive question "Are you my mother?" Peter said that as a child he felt like that little bird, looking for where he belonged, expecting to find a surrogate mother somewhere outside his abusive home.

The savior myth, in adulthood, has implications for unrealistic expectations of significant others and resultant disappointment in relationships and marriage. The savior or rescuer turns out to be human, with his or her own faults and limitations, and the pain of the survivor still throbs. The myth spreads beyond relationships to an unrealistic hope in a deus ex machina, a resolution of conflicts, struggle, and pain from outside. Kate described the expectation this way: "I feel like I'm at a dead end, waiting for someone to build a road."

The Myth of Normalcy

Young children tend to view their own experience as normative, unaware that other families might not function in the same way. Their experience is what they know, and what they know feels normal.

In older years, children begin to see differences between their home and the homes of their friends. His best friend sleeps with not one but two sheets on his bed; her neighbor's father mows their lawn regularly; her classmates have a regular bedtime; his friend's father plays ball with them. The older child begins to develop a sense of something he or she calls "normal," which in the child's mind means the way families are supposed to be and the way most other families are. With this belief in normalcy comes a sense of shame within the child, a vague conviction of something being wrong with her or him.

Mat looked to the *Donna Reed Show* as his model for normalcy, and he often pretended to friends that his family fit that form. He developed an image of himself based on what he believed normal was, yet he always felt like a fraud. The myth of normalcy helped him fit in with friends while growing up but left him having no idea who he really was as an adult.

The implications for adulthood of the normalcy myth are a sense of shame regarding oneself, deep aloneness (because no one can know who the adult child really is), and an "as if" quality to one's life (the adult child also not knowing who she or he really is). The myth of normalcy sets the stage for difficulties with intimacy, as the myth holder is not able to open up and be vulnerable with others, not able to risk trust. Mat voiced a refrain often spoken by survivors of childhood trauma: "If people knew who I really am, they wouldn't like me."

The Myth of Restoration

Children have an uncanny capacity to hope, even in the face of overwhelming evidence that hope is unwarranted. Just as children of divorced parents hope for their parents to reconcile, even after the parents are remarried to other partners, children in dysfunctional families often hold fast to a hope that things will turn around and peace will be restored. The hope takes various forms: "Maybe this Thanksgiving will be different and Dad won't get drunk"; "Maybe the new pills will keep Mom from getting depressed"; "Maybe when my stepbrother finds a girlfriend he won't make me touch him anymore"; "Maybe my parents will stop fighting now that they got another car." The myth of restoration is a prayer that something is going to change and everyone will be happy again (even when there is no memory of happiness in the past).

Peter remembered a cruelly violent episode that took place when he was a preschooler. His father beat his mother almost to unconsciousness, as four-year-old Peter looked on. As his mother whimpered in the fetal position on the kitchen floor, Peter went to his father and hugged him. He steadfastly believed that peace could be restored in his family.

In adulthood, the myth of restoration leaves the individual reaching out time and again to dysfunctional family members with expectations of healthy interaction, arranging family get-togethers, contriving heart-to-heart talks. The individual somehow trusts that everything will work out and be all right as long as everyone shares his or her feelings, as long as the family spends quality time together, or as long as everyone tries hard and works together for healing. The adult child sometimes has difficulty understanding and accepting that healing is her or his own individual responsibility and that it entails differentiation from the family rather than enmeshed reconciliation of the family. The implications in adulthood of the myth of restoration are a denial of the insidious nature of family dysfunction and a lack of responsibility for one's present-day functioning.

Peter struggled with his family for months to try to effect restoration, with phone calls to his brothers communicating a desire to spend more time together and conversations with his parents about what needed to change in the family dynamics for them to be close as a family. He confronted his father regarding past abuse, in the hope of getting his father to see the pain he caused the family and to apologize, thereby facilitating healing. Peter's brothers told him they were busy with their own lives; his parents felt they were already close as a family; and his father insisted his behavior could not be categorized as "abuse." The family resented his attempts to heal them. In letting go of the myth of restoration with his family of origin, Peter channeled his energy more fully into his marriage and into developing his parenting skills.

METHOD

In moving toward wholeness and healing, the survivor has the task of demythologizing, of moving beyond the myths—which in adulthood serve no longer as sacred stories but as pretenses—to a functional theology of hope and authentic restoration. Rudolf Bultmann, who originally coined the term "demythologizing," speaks of the necessity of demythologizing in Christian spirituality: "Let us abandon the mythological conceptions precisely because we want to retain their deeper meaning. . . . [Demythologizing's] aim is not to eliminate the mythological statements but to interpret them."[2]

The myths of adult children hold within them the power of hope, of trust in the goodness of creation, and of redemption. As such, the myths hold spiritual value, even into adulthood. The theologically developed response to the myths includes letting go of false conceptions of salvation and taking on an understanding of the element of the divine in wholeness and restoration.

Connecting with the Child

Often the adult's memory of childhood imposes adult selfhood and culpability onto the child. It is hard for an adult to have memory of her or his degree of consciousness and verbal understanding at a given age in childhood, so the adult remembers images that can be hard to separate from her or his current sense of awareness.

Part of the process of demythologizing, for the adult child, includes a connection with the historical child to gain new perspective of the child's experience and views. The survivor of childhood wounding needs to understand the historic child as truly being a child. In memory work, the survivor needs to recognize that as a child, he or she was dependent, powerless to control much of his or her environment, unsophisticated, vulnerable, and good (in terms of personhood).

Identifying with a Child. The caregiver can facilitate connection with the historic child through helping the parishioner to identify with a child in her or his current life. The survivor might bring to mind a child of her or his own gender who is the same age as the survivor was when much of the trauma happened. This child might be a relative (a niece, nephew, daughter, son, or grandchild), a friend's child, or a fictional child from a television program or from a book.

With a child in mind, the careseeker is encouraged to describe that child using adjectives. Carefree, out to conquer the world, mischievous, loving, trusting, full of life, innocent, vulnerable, affectionate, and dependent are examples of adjectives individuals may draw on in describing a child they have in mind. The adult child can then be asked to identify with the present child, to recognize that as an eight-year-old she too had many of the same qualities; that as a preschooler he too was trusting, affectionate, and out to conquer the world. Since often the survivor has never thought of himself or herself in the way he or she thinks of a child in his or her life today, this part of the connection can be quite cathartic.

After the parishioner has completed the exercise of identifying with the child, the pastoral caregiver needs to guide her or him through questions such as, "How would it affect this child if he lost his father now?" "Can you imagine what it would be like for this child to be raised by an alcoholic mother?" and "If this child were assaulted by her grandfather, would you think she was to blame?" The questions can be formulated by drawing on what the pastor knows of the survivor's childhood history and of the myths the survivor holds.

Sarah struggled with blaming herself for her father's and her grandfather's sexual abuse of her as a small child. She identified with her niece, a spunky, trusting, eager child who was the same age Sarah was when her abuse started. When asked if she would blame her niece if her niece were sexually assaulted, Sarah adamantly said, "Of course not!" Although Sarah could not allow herself to be angry with her perpetrators for their abuse of her, she stated that she would want to kill anyone who tried to touch her niece.

Using Photographs in Demythologizing. The parishioner can also bring in photographs of herself or himself as a child, as an exercise in connecting with the historical child. To look at the child in the picture, to reflect on what is seen, and to listen to the pastor's observations can also facilitate an understanding of the historical child as a child.

When Peter brought in photographs, he was astonished to see that the pictures of himself as a toddler showed a smiling, happy face, whereas pictures of himself from preschool years on up showed a stiffness and fear. (It was after his toddler years that Peter's father had returned from the Korean War and had acted out his unintegrated combat trauma through domestic violence.)

Connecting with the historical child is an initial step in demythologizing, as it allows the adult child the opportunity to step back from, and begin to develop more objectivity toward, the experience.

Dialoguing about the Myths

When the stage has been set, with the parishioner beginning to view her or his childhood through a different lens, the pastoral caregiver continues in demythologizing by challenging the myths. In dialogue about each myth, the pastor prods, uses humor, plays devil's advocate, and feigns ignorance in confronting the usefulness of the myth. The examples listed earlier in this chapter for each of the common myths of survivors of childhood trauma illustrate these caregiver techniques.

The Myth of the Good Parent. With the myth of the good parent, the pastor needs to convey the message that maybe the parent just wasn't a good parent and (if the parent is still living) probably never will be a good parent. The following interchange occurred in response to Jean's agony regarding her father's rejections:

> PASTOR: Maybe he's just not a good father.
> JEAN: But he is! He really loves us. He's always told us that.
> PASTOR: What if he loves you but just doesn't know how to be a good father?
> JEAN: But I'm sure he wants to be a good father.
> PASTOR: But it doesn't sound like he is. He didn't tell you he was moving?
> JEAN: (After silence.) No, he didn't tell me he was moving.
> PASTOR: Your father may never be the father you wish he could be.

The Myth of Control. The pastoral caregiver challenges the myth of control with the message that there was nothing the adult child could have done to "fix things." In response to Jean's insistence that she could have done something as a child to keep her father from constantly leaving, the following pastoral dialogue ensued:

> PASTOR: So you think he left because the house wasn't spotless?
> JEAN: No, but ...
> PASTOR: Because you didn't give him enough pictures from art class?
> JEAN: No, but ...
> PASTOR: Because you couldn't keep them [Jean's parents] from fighting?
> JEAN: Yes! If things had been more peaceful around the house, I'm sure he would've stayed.
> PASTOR: You think so?
> JEAN: Yes!
> PASTOR: Why was it your job to keep them from fighting?
> JEAN: Because they didn't have control over it.
> PASTOR: But you did?
>
> (Silence.)
>
> PASTOR: Remember that little girl in church school you identified with? Do you think she could keep her parents from fighting if one drank heavily and left home for months at a time?
> JEAN: No. I don't know why I think I had that power.

The Savior Myth. The caregiver, in response to the savior myth, challenges with the question, "What if no one ever comes to rescue you?" Kate's metaphor of feeling like she's at a dead end waiting for someone to build the road elicited this dialogue:

> Pastor: What if no one builds that road?
> Kate: I know. I don't really think anyone ever will. I feel stuck.
> Pastor: Maybe you have to build your own road.
> Kate: (Laughs.) Yes! Or turn around and find a different way!

The Myth of Normalcy. The myth of normalcy is challenged by questioning the meaning of "normal." In response to Mat's wistful vision of Donna Reed, this pastoral interchange occurred:

> PASTOR: Do you really think Donna Reed was a normal mom?
> MAT: (Laughs) No, she certainly wasn't. I don't think people are really like that.
> PASTOR: What do you think of as normal?
> MAT: Well, a nice house with a picket fence, two and a half kids, a two-car garage, and a dog. I've got the dog!
> PASTOR: Your idea of normal sounds pretty superficial to me.
> MAT: (Laughs again.) Yeah, to me too. Maybe normal just means being able to be myself.

The Myth of Restoration. The pastoral challenge to the myth of restoration holds out the probability that the family dysfunction will never change. This pastoral intervention occurred upon Peter's frustration at his efforts to get his family together:

> Pastor: Sounds like they don't want to be fixed.
> Peter: No, you're right. They like things just as they are. Status quo. They don't know any different. I don't know why I keep trying to change them. I think I know that's just the way they are. But maybe I haven't really accepted that.
> Pastor: It's hard to let go of that hope that things could be different.
> Peter: Yes. I didn't want my parents to be right.
> Pastor: You didn't want your parents to be right?
> Peter: Yes. They always said that life is hard. And they live that way too: like life is a burden. Maybe they're right. I didn't want them to be, but maybe they're right. Life is hard.

Postmythology

The process of letting go of the childhood survivor myths leaves the parishioner in the enviable position of rebuilding a worldview based on hope wrested from the experience of suffering, rather than hope based on denial of the experience of suffering, or on the premise that the experience is not as it seems. The task of demythologizing is not to blow apart the hope that has kept the individual going, but to peel away the myth in order to come to a faith-based (as opposed to a defensive) hope. (Chapters 8 and 9 of this book address the development of a sense of restoration and hope that transcends psychological defenses.) As Bultmann observes in regard to the work of demythologizing the New Testament,

> Demythologizing is the radical application of the doctrine of justification by faith to the sphere of knowledge and thought.... Demythologizing destroys every longing for security.... [The one] who abandons every form of security will find the true security. [The individual] before God has always empty hands.[3]

chapter five

Breaking the Silence, Telling the Story

> If we do not claim the soul's power on our own behalf, we become its victims. We suffer our emotions rather than feel them working for us. We hold our thoughts and passions inward, disconnecting them from life, and then they stir up trouble within, making us feel profoundly unsettled or, it seems, turning into illness.
> —Thomas Moore, *Care of the Soul*

Many adult survivors of childhood wounding carry memories of trauma, neglect, and abuse that they have never before shared with another. Some hold on to these memories as their darkest secrets, feeling that this dark history is shameful and untouchable.

For the victim-survivor, telling the story is critical in "claim[ing] the soul's power on [one's] own behalf" through the healing of past wounds. Breaking the silence breaks the bonds of shame. Sharing with another eases the sense of aloneness. Voicing the pain undams the river of hope. This chapter addresses the ending of silence from a pastoral perspective.

THEORY AND BACKGROUND

Ending the silence has a profound impact on the spirit of the individual: his or her capacity to relate to others, repertoire of feeling, consciousness of self, sense of freedom and responsibility, intellect, and connection with the divine in human life.

The Spirit of the Secret-Bearer

More often than not, the trauma that the wounded adult child has experienced has never been fully disclosed to another. Although sometimes the victim-survivor has confided in one or two close friends about some degree of the abuse, the story has usually never been fully exposed to the light of interpersonal revelation.

A tremendous step toward healing from past trauma is made with the telling of the story. The pastoral caregiver is sometimes the first professional trusted with the sharing, the pastor or rabbi being viewed by many as safe and nonjudgmental.

For the most part, not talking, not trusting, and not sharing have been functional defenses for the adult child, given the family environment. The secrecy protects the ego and personhood (intelligence, feeling, self-awareness, interpersonal connectedness, and measure of freedom) of the child. To give up the secret is to leave oneself vulnerable to judgment and to further pain.

For one to hold a secret means to keep oneself a degree apart from others (since there is this thing one knows that others cannot know); it means battling with shame, using psychic energy to maintain the boundaries of the secret, and struggling without the input of collective wisdom while trying to make meaning out of something that defies sense.

Intimacy with Others. Barbara spent hours in pastoral counseling in agonizing silence. She would begin to tell something of the sexual abuse by her uncle, but then she would clam up. She would literally open her mouth and start to force out a sound, only to close her mouth and bow her head in defeat. She became paralyzed at the thought of telling her story. Barbara feared that disclosure of her sexual abuse would adversely affect the pastoral relationship. Although she could not share the details, Barbara did share the duration (several years), the intensity (her uncle was cruel, sadistically hurting her in his sexual molestation), and the impact of her abuse (she was unable to make close friends with women, unable even to conceive of an intimate relationship with a man, unable to sleep at night without a light on in her room and without the door bolted, and unable to feel at peace in the world).

Holding on to the secret perpetuates for the survivor an isolation of that which is deep and sacred within. The survivor experiences a sense of being different from others, a sense of being alone with the pain, and a difficulty trusting others with closeness. Telling the story to another who cares, especially to a professional who is trained to offer empathy, to provide safety, and to reframe the meaning wrested from the experience, can considerably heal a person's ability to relate to and to trust others.

Battling Shame. Maxine grew up in rural poverty, without plumbing or running water. As a teenager she lived a "double life," feeling happy and normal at school and disgusted at home. She left for secretarial school at eighteen and eventually settled down in another state. When Maxine first disclosed, in a pastoral support group, the conditions of her childhood home, she felt suffused with shame. She was surprised when other members of the group felt empathy rather than disgust toward her after she shared her story.

Victim-survivors hold a unique shame. Being wounded is a debasement of the self. Simply being involved in domestic trauma sets one up for a sense of being existentially unanchored; the home is supposed to be a haven of safety, a sanctuary from the outside world, not an environment of trauma and dysfunction. Sharing the story of the childhood domestic trauma lessens the shame (which is closely tied to the myth of normalcy), as the hearer responds with empathy, caring, and acceptance, rather than with the feared judgment or rejection. When the interpersonal relationship is not damaged but enhanced through disclosure in a safe setting, the adult child loses some of the feeling that something is wrong with him or her.

A degree of the shame stems from simply being the bearer of a secret, from keeping the silence about an injustice that should be screamed. For the adult child to tell just one receptive person about the wounding events and about the people involved in these events is to lessen that debilitating shame.

Redirecting Psychic Energy. After Peter initially shared his memories of childhood abuse by his Korean-vet father, he described feeling a tremendous release: "It's not that I felt depressed before or anything, but I feel so much lighter now. It's literally like a weight has been lifted."

To bear memory that one feels should not be shared with another entails a labor of the mind; the mind sets apart and holds at bay that memory, which nevertheless is always dancing at the background of awareness. The labor is not a one-time effort, even in the case of repression (where traumatic events are stored outside of conscious memory); it is a continuous effort of containment. Although this labor is usually not a process the victim-survivor is aware of, nonetheless it necessitates an expense of psychic energy.

With the sharing of traumatic memories comes a catharsis, a spilling out and letting go of stored emotion. The sharing of traumatic memory can be experienced as an emotional and a psychological cleansing. The energy redirected through no longer bearing the secret often results in a broadened repertoire of feeling and a heightened sense of consciousness of oneself. Following a disclosure, over many weeks, of traumatic childhood memories of her older brother's schizophrenia, Katie described feeling like a newborn baby, experiencing emotions that felt entirely new to her, and having an awareness of herself as if for the first time.

Meaning Making. Peter had tried to make sense for himself out of his experience of prolonged childhood domestic violence. He had asked questions along the lines of "Why did God let this happen?" and had developed a fairly complex theological understanding of the abuse. He had come to view the domestic violence as a punishment from God for his father's having killed others in war. His father had been, in a sense, cursed, and his children cursed as well, to live in a hell of violence.

When the question was raised whether the "curse" was being passed to Peter's children—was Peter abusive to them?—Peter responded, "No, by the grace of God." Peter believed that if he did not get close to his children, they would be spared the curse. He circumvented the passing on of the abuse by avoiding intimacy with his children.

Being unable to talk with anyone regarding his own history of domestic violence, Peter had not the gift of the wisdom and experience of others in developing meaning out of his childhood trauma. After his disclosure of the violence, he revamped his theology of suffering into one in which God was not the reason behind the abuse but rather the agent of restoration.

Judith Herman writes,

> Reconstructing the trauma story also includes a systematic review of the meaning of the event, both to the patient and to the important people in her life. The traumatic event challenges an ordinary person to become a theologian, a philosopher, and a jurist. The survivor is called upon to articulate the values and beliefs that she once held and that the trauma destroyed. She stands mute before the emptiness of evil, feeling the insufficiency of any known system of explanation. Survivors of atrocity of every age and every culture come to a point in their testimony where all questions are reduced to one, spoken more in bewilderment than in outrage: Why? The answer is beyond human understanding.[1]

For the victim-survivor to tell the pastoral caregiver the story of her or his abuse is to open up to pastoral input and pastoral interpretation of the experience, and to affirm the work of the holy in the meaning-making process.

The Politics of Secrecy

Dayl Hufford makes the searing statement that "child sexual abuse occurs because secrecy and silence nurture the abuse in the home and in society. They are needed for child sexual abuse to continue.

Revealing the secret and breaking the silence can change this."[2] Hufford's words are equally true for physical abuse, for alcoholism in the family, and for other forms of domestic trauma. Secrecy and silence shield dysfunction from the light of collective wisdom. How shocked our society has been in recent decades to realize the pervasiveness of alcoholism, domestic violence, and sexual abuse of children. The occurrence of family dysfunction has long been guarded through a complicit code of silence.

For survivors to tell the story and break the silence regarding domestic trauma is to pass on information that needs to be shared for collective survival, just as people need to communicate regarding the catastrophic trauma of famine, war, or natural disaster. As a receiver of stories of pain, trauma, and abuse, the pastoral caregiver is in a position to serve as a prophet. Although the minister holds the stories protectively, folding them up and taking them into her or his own soul, the minister also registers the information about family dysfunction and how it affects lives. The caregiver connects the information with other stories of victim-survivors and makes an integrated meaning of the pain.

The meaning making refines and informs the carer's pastoral theology and practical theology. The theology and the meaning are returned to the community through informational education, dialogue with other professionals, and subsequent pastoral care.

Method

For some survivors, the story is easy to tell verbally and chronologically. For others, the story is something of a puzzle, with gaps in memory here or questions about time line there. It is not unusual for survivors to have difficulty in verbalizing their history and their hurt. The duration and intensity of the abuse are often directly correlated to the difficulty with which the story is told, as well as to the degree of repression.

It is not unusual for adult survivors of childhood domestic trauma to have impairments in memory. The impairment often indicates the extent of emotional trauma in the history; the difficulty in remembering is protective, a repression and a denial that protect the self from the blow of the trauma. The gaps in memory can serve as a cushion, an amnesiac sac that enables the self to feel somewhat safe and trusting in a world that has been hostile.

Some adult children have already shared their history with a trusted friend or partner, yet often without the full feeling that accompanies the trauma. For these individuals it is still helpful to tell the story to the pastoral counselor, for further integration of feeling and meaning as well as for the pastoral input of the caregiver. Often with each new telling of the story, the parishioner becomes aware of his or her growth and healing since the initial disclosure and receives new insight.

The telling of the story may happen in one sitting, yet more often it is a process of gradual disclosure, from general to more detailed, from objectified to more feeling-laden, over time.

Direct Narrative

For the victim-survivor whose memories are accessible and who can tolerate the pain of sharing the story, the minister provides the gift of being a witness (as described in chapter 2), walking the road of memory with the parishioner, and offering empathy and acceptance. The only intervention the witness needs to make is to mirror the experience, to reflect back the feelings and perceptions of the historical child. The more the victim-survivor is able to feel as she or he shares the memories, the greater are the catharsis and the opportunity for reintegration. Mirroring comments would include, "You must have been very frightened," "That sounds so painful," or "As a little boy, you felt lost, even abandoned."

Interpretation by the pastoral caregiver is unnecessary and can even distract from the narrative. Asking questions such as "What happened next?" or "What did you do then?" can also be unhelpful, in that informational questions have a tendency to steer the adult child away from feelings.

The pastoral caregiver also needs to refrain from challenging the memory. There may indeed be times when the caregiver is incredulous of the memories being reported, perhaps not wanting to believe the horror described, perhaps sensing something inauthentic in the parishioner's manner of telling, or perhaps protecting himself or herself from the pain of empathy with one who has suffered profound trauma.

Many survivors of childhood trauma fear not being believed and sometimes relay that anxiety in the communication of the story, so that the words and feelings do not seem to fit and, consequently, seem to convey a quality of inauthenticity. Other survivors struggle with acceptance of their history, going back and forth from disbelieving to trusting their memories. As Mary described it, "I feel like I have a little man on each shoulder, one saying, 'This really happened,' and the other saying, 'You made this up!'" As adult children battle their own doubts, the pastoral counselor may also tend to doubt the history.

The pastoral caregiver needs to communicate an openness to hearing what the parishioner is sharing, and a respect for the individual. The caregiver should mentally note his or her feelings of doubt or outright disbelief, but to challenge the veracity of the adult child's story at this point could be counterproductive and even damaging.

Writing

The victim-survivor can also be encouraged to write an autobiography of her or his childhood. Writing serves the multiple functions of confirming the significance of the trauma, validating feelings, bringing about catharsis, and making meaning.

For the careseeker who is unable to share memories verbally, autobiographical writing can be an alternate way to break the silence. Barbara, who felt paralyzed to talk about her history, was able to write in her journal about some of the memories and to share the writing in the counseling hour. One entry began, "When I sit with you, I wish I could answer your questions and talk about things. I remember how it all started, but after that it all runs together." The entry continued, describing events of horror and cruelty that Barbara could not share verbally.

Sharing and Gathering Information from Family Members

In several ways, turning to benevolent family and extended family members can be helpful in breaking the silence and telling the story. First, being able to share the story with someone who knows something of the situation can add to catharsis and healing. Family members can validate memories, easing the debilitating doubt. Family members can also shed light on unanswered questions.

Judy, who was adopted as a child and constantly fantasized about her "real" mother coming to rescue her, spoke with her older brother (a biological child of her parents) about her memories of both parents being rigid and strict to the point of being abusive. Although she had feared talking with her brother about the family history, her brother welcomed the conversation. "Yes," he confirmed, "they were terrible parents." Judy's brother reminded her of an incident she had not thought about in decades: her parents locked her in her bedroom as a young adolescent to keep her from seeing a boy they didn't like. Her father, a pharmacist, heavily sedated her to keep her inside the house.

Judy felt gratitude following the talk with her brother. She felt validated, relieved that he agreed with her perception of the family, and she felt closer to him after the conversation.

It should be noted that sharing with other family members often brings to light more information, which may be overwhelming for a parishioner already laden with unintegrated experience. Sharing secrets can bring to light deeper secrets. Some survivors find it hard to take in knowledge of even further dysfunction within their family; they need to have solid support networks in place to process additional pieces of the puzzle. Mention should also be made that often family members, even benevolent ones, are averse to "airing the family's dirty laundry" or "dwelling on the past." The defenses of these family members should be respected.

Retrieving Memory

Linda Meyer Williams conducted research surveying 129 adult women who, as children, had been treated at hospital emergency rooms after being molested. The study found that 38 percent of the women did not remember the trauma. Of the 80 women who remembered the abuse, some said there had been a time when they had forgotten it.[3]

"The retrieval and validation of repressed memories has an important role in the recovery process," write Judith Herman and Emily Schatzow. "With the return of memory, the patient has an opportunity as an adult to integrate an experience that was beyond her capacity to endure as a child. . . . The relief of particular post-traumatic symptoms following recovery of memory is often dramatic."[4]

A number of victim-survivors may have gaps in memory, with a vague, uneasy sense of what these gaps may contain. Some may find retrieval of memory difficult. For the parishioner who has embarked on an earnest journey to know and remember more, several techniques can facilitate the process.

Note should be made that repressed memory work should not be done by an untrained professional, as the flooding of emotion accompanying the return of repressed memory can be overwhelming for the survivor. The pastoral caregiver should do memory work only in conjunction with a mental health care provider specializing in trauma work.

Referral to a Support Group or a Therapy Group. The use of a support group made up of other victim-survivors in a recovery process often prompts remembering for the victim-survivor who has gaps in memory. Hearing the story of another can trigger retrieval of traumatic history, as can simply listening to the intense feelings of another in healing.

Joan and Julie, participants in a women's group for adult children of dysfunctional families, both felt strongly that there was sexual abuse in their history, although neither had conscious memory of sexual abuse. They identified with each other, being of a similar age, being divorced, and having grown children. Their work together facilitated retrieval of memory for both of them, as each received courage and strength from the other.

When Joan spoke of her terror of remembering any more trauma, Julie felt the same terror echo within herself. Joan's terror was connected with her alcoholic father, who in her conscious memory had physically abused her. Julie's terror also centered on her abusive father; accompanying her terror, she began to experience images of the cellar of her childhood home. Joan and Julie drew support from each other as they falteringly put together pieces of their childhood experience.

Bibliotherapy. The survivor might be referred to a book relating a story of domestic trauma, or to a movie that tells the story of one who grew up in a dysfunctional home. Britanny's memories of being molested as a preschooler by a church school teacher flooded her after viewing a made-for-television movie. She said that as a child she had remembered the molestation, but had not remembered it since adolescence. After reading the autobiography of an actress raised in an alcoholic family, Marcus remembered a few more incidents from his alcoholic childhood home.

Photographs. The careseeker can be encouraged to bring in photographs from childhood and to talk about what he or she remembers from the time and what he or she has been told about the photographs.

Joan routinely became severely depressed around Hanukkah. She began to wonder whether something might have happened on this holiday. When she brought in photographs of the family Hanukkah traditions, she was struck by one from which her mother was absent. Joan recalled having been told that when she was young, her mother had been in the hospital for several weeks with complications following the birth of her sister, including the period of Hanukkah. She wondered aloud who had taken care of her during that time. (Her father, from before her birth until his death from kidney failure when Joan was seventeen, had been a severe alcoholic.)

Over several weeks following the sharing of the photographs, Joan experienced flashbacks of her father in the bathroom, hurting her. She eventually pieced together a memory of her father molesting her in the bathtub as a small child. She guessed the trauma had happened when her mother was in the hospital during the period of Hanukkah.

Focusing on What Is Remembered. Often helpful in retrieval of memory is a focus on what is remembered, on details that are accessible. Julie felt deathly afraid of her cellar as a child. The cellar was dark, dank, and dirty. She described the staircase into the cellar, the coal burner in the corner, the shelves of goods canned by her mother, the bin of onions and potatoes. As she described these things, Julie gave a start as she suddenly remembered a cistern in the cellar, in which several large snakes had once bedded. This memory prompted another memory: her father, wanting Julie to overcome her fear of snakes, had killed the snakes and hung them from the clothesline for a week. Her father then ordered her to take the dead snakes to school for show-and-tell. Her refusal prompted a beating.

Free-Association Writing. Memory is sometimes not so much technically repressed as simply not remembered for a considerable length of time (as in the "I had forgotten about that!" experience of one who has not thought of a certain incident for ages). For retrieval of this sort of memory, free-association writing is helpful. The parishioner can be encouraged to keep a journal in which he or she writes whatever comes to mind regarding childhood, particularly painful, enraging, shameful, confusing, or sad events. Free-association writing can call to mind past wounding that the adult child has not yet integrated simply because she or he has not paid attention to it.

False Memory Syndrome

A mention should be made of a phenomenon called "false memory syndrome." The proponents of false memory theory hold that, although the frequency of occurrence is unclear, some individuals become the victims of overly zealous mental health professionals who lead them to believe they are survivors of abuse that never actually occurred. The false memory theory has been applied primarily to those who believe they have recovered repressed memory of childhood sexual abuse. The pastoral caregiver can avoid this phenomenon by following the parishioner's lead in pastoral care memory work and by laying aside any hunches as to what might lie in the childhood history of the parishioner.

False memory theorists also challenge the ethics of using hypnosis, truth serum, or guided imagery in memory work with clients, asserting that clients can be highly vulnerable to suggestion by trusted therapists. Because pastoral caregivers do not use truth serum in their work and because few pastors are trained in the use of hypnosis, the main caution would be against using guided imagery with careseekers. Guided imagery should not be used as a means for a parishioner to access memory, but rather as a vehicle for resolution and healing of conscious wounds (as is further discussed in chapters 7, 8, and 9).

CONCLUSION

In bearing witness and giving testimony to their suffering, adult survivors make a significant step in healing, "claim[ing] the soul's power on [their] own behalf." The pastoral caregiver, in witnessing, receiving, and respecting the story, offers validity, empathy, and hope to one whose suffering has been exposed to its own painful truth.

The pastoral carer, unique among caregivers in representing the sacred, is able to be like Annie Dillard's mountain for the wounded adult child: "Mountains are giant, restful, absorbent. You can heave your spirit into a mountain and the mountain will keep it, folded, and not throw it back as some creeks will. The mountains are home."[5] The caregiver receives the story, respects the telling, and quietly participates in the sacred unfolding of meaning.

chapter six

Confronting Wounders of the Past

> Directing the anger at the source of the suffering is vital if a victim is to be able to move through the process of recovery and healing. There may be multiple sources: initially, the offender, and, secondarily, the system which may have been nonsupportive or even further victimized the victim. A victim's anger as a healthy and appropriate response to victimization motivates the victim to act on her/his own behalf. When it is directed outward towards the appropriate source, it energizes the victim.
> —Marie Fortune, *Sexual Violence*

Often adult children, as part of the recovery process, feel the need to break the silence with the offending or abusive parent or other abusive family member. Following through on this need can be productive and healthy for the victim-survivor. This chapter focuses on confrontation with living offenders, whereas chapter 7 focuses on confrontation with deceased figures of the past, or with living perpetrators with whom direct confrontation feels physically or emotionally unsafe.

THEORY AND BACKGROUND

With the task of confrontation, the survivor enters an interactive, dynamic phase of recovery. The parental response to the challenge and the subsequent realignment and readjustment of worldview, view of self, and view of others, which the victim-survivor needs to make, are critical in healing. The dynamic of confrontation triggers increased awareness of the limitations of the offender and increased differentiation from the dysfunctional family, and offers the opportunity for further integration of value paradoxes and for increased demythologizing.

Parental Defenses

Because parents and guardians usually hold to a belief that they have done their best with child rearing, when adult children confront their parents with the perception that they've been hurt, wounded, or damaged by a dysfunctional childhood, the parents are likely to avoid accepting this challenge. More often than not, the avoiding response is not conscious but is, rather, an unconscious defense that all the reasoning and honesty the confronter draws upon will not crack.

Karen wrote her mother a letter telling of her process of recovery and suggesting that her mother and father's rigid, moralizing, and critical religious views had left her feeling that she could never be good enough. She said she longed for acceptance and support from her parents. She received a one-page letter back from her mother. The letter read:

> Dear Karen,
> [entire page blank]
>   Mom

The parental response provides the careseeker with the opportunity to acknowledge and accept the limitations of the parents, paradoxically allowing the adult child further growth and healing as the individual begins to take increasing responsibility for moving beyond the woundedness.

Differentiation

Any family system entails a degree of enmeshment between family members, a certain shared identity with diffuse boundaries. As a child grows, the enmeshment lessens with the child developing increased identity and increased sense of self apart from the family system. Differentiation is the process of separating from the system through a healthy development of a free and responsible self.

Differentiation from a dysfunctional family is a challenge, since the family dynamics do not include all the elements that make for healthy growing up. Codependency and the adult child characteristics of harsh judgment of self, difficulty with intimate relationships, exceeding loyalty, and the feeling of being different all tend to keep the victim-survivor enmeshed, to a degree, with the family of origin. Although the dysfunctional family may be fraught with pain, it is a familiar pain. Michael Kerr writes:

> Keep in mind that the person working towards a better level of differentiation is working against powerful emotional forces within him/herself that say, "If you do this, it will seriously threaten his/her acceptance and approval of you, and will leave you feeling you have not met your responsibility for his/her happiness and well-being." At the same time, the person making the effort is being told these things by other family members. It is never easy to sustain the effort and the family members will never support and encourage it, since they are too locked in themselves.[1]

The careseeker has the task in healing of developing increased identity and sense of self apart from the dysfunctional family. The by-product of differentiation is increased self-confidence, increased sense of self-worth, and increased willingness to take responsibility for one's life.

After writing her letter to her mother, Karen continued to try to talk with her parents, only to receive condemnation and moralizing from the staunchly religious couple. Karen tried dialogue with her father, a deacon in his church and a man well versed in scripture and theology. She spoke about grace, unconditional love, and the gospel of resurrection, whereas he spoke about judgment, God's hating the sinner, and the Second Coming of Christ.

Karen came to the slow awareness that her father and mother were not going to soften their religious views, even in the interest of their only daughter's mental health. She used the understanding as an occasion to challenge her own faith, coming to a strong trust in God's grace. She took the symbolic step of joining the local mainline Protestant church she had been attending, confidently differentiating herself from her Pentecostal upbringing. She read spiritual writings voraciously, enjoying the freedom to challenge and refine her own understanding of a theology of grace.

Value Paradoxes and Confrontation

Confrontation with the wounder enforces through action the integration of value paradoxes. Healthy encounter draws on an authentic selfhood, on assertion of feelings, and on self-affirmation.

Even as an adult child is able to experience differentiation and freedom in other important areas of her or his life, often the setting of the family of origin is still a relentless polarizer for any remaining unresolved conflict. The family of origin is one of the last strongholds of a recovering adult survivor's dysfunctional dynamics. For the victim-survivor to be able to successfully practice selfhood, assertiveness, and self-affirmation within the dysfunctional family setting reinforces and validates the healing spirit. The following example reflects the servanthood-versus-selfhood and meekness-versus-assertiveness struggles.

Peter's mother, on one of his visits, asked Peter (the man, described in chapter 4, who as a child loved the book *Are You My Mother?*) to move a nest of bird eggs from a lower branch of the tree in the front yard to one of the highest branches. She feared the neighborhood kids would find the nest and disturb the eggs. Peter argued with his mother that moving the nest itself could disturb the eggs, but her plaintive anxiety prevailed. Against his better judgment, Peter climbed the tree and delicately moved the nest to a higher branch. Later that afternoon, Peter saw with remorse that the nest had fallen to the sidewalk, and the eggs had cracked.

Peter, who had been working on issues of assertiveness in therapy, saw this incident as a clarion call to change. He, who had been afraid of hurting his mother, afraid of her fragility, and afraid of his own anger, sat down with his mother the next week to challenge her silent complicity in his father's physical abuse of Peter and his siblings. Despite his mother's whimpering that she did not feel strong enough to talk about it, Peter voiced his dreaded suspicion that, when his father had taken out his wrath on him and the other children, his mother had been relieved that it wasn't her.

Peter expressed a determination to listen to his own best judgment in the future, not simply to accede to others' wishes and needs. He said, "I know now that I have to trust myself."

Victim-Survivor Myths and Confrontation

Confrontation with the offender also enforces, through action, the demythologizing of victim-survivor myths. The challenge to the careseeker entails breaking through a blind hope that the dysfunction is not what it seems. The response of the caretakers often breaks through the survivor's false belief that these authority figures are capable of good, loving parenting, or the unrealistic expectation that the adult child can change them.

The Myth of the Good Parent. Confrontation provides the parent with an opportunity to respond to the adult child with love, support, and acceptance. Often the parishioner, in spite of his or her best awareness, will hope for a loving, healthy, even repentant response from the parent. Usually, though, the encounter will instead bring the adult survivor of childhood wounding to the realization that his or her parents are who they are—individuals with limitations and weaknesses, stuck in dysfunction.

Peter, after his confrontation with his mother, said, "She just can't be who I want her to be. I really don't think she'll ever be able to love me the way I wish she could."

The Myth of Control. A confrontation often leaves the careseeker with a sense of impotence that is paradoxically freeing. The challenge enables the adult child to come to terms with her or his lack of power to change the dysfunctional system.

Karen, following the dialogue with her father, voiced an insight that there was nothing she could do to make her parents accept her: "It's not even about me. They just live in a different world, where everything is black and white, right or wrong. And since they believe humans to be worthless, depraved, and sinful, I can never be okay. But it's not just me: no one can be."

The Savior Myth. A confrontation challenges the savior myth through the resultant differentiation of self, which leads the individual to abandon hope in a rescuer and move toward welcomed acceptance of responsibility for his or her own life.

Judy confronted her adoptive mother with being verbally abusive, only to meet a flurry of confusion and hurt from her mother. Around the same time, she had located her birth mother through an adoption search agency. Her birth mother turned out to be a drifter who had never made much of her life. Judy, rather than feeling crushed that this would-be rescuer herself needed more rescuing than Judy would ever be able to provide, felt a freedom. "Since I've confronted my mother," she said, "I've felt like I don't need anyone to save me anymore. I feel like I want to try to be my own mother to myself."

The Myth of Normalcy. When one consciously challenges, as an adult, the wounding of childhood, the act serves as a form of reality testing. The challenge is a way of saying, "Yes, this happened. And no, this was not normal."

Anne Wilson Schaef challenges those who would effect a shift from dysfunctional thinking to "see what you see, and know what you know."[2] The task is to move beyond denial or minimization of dysfunction and instead to open one's eyes in objective assessment.

David (chapter 1), in talking with his father about his mother's manic-depressive illness, was startled that his father kept insisting that his mother was fine. David pointed out several instances when his mother had not acted mentally fit, yet each time his father responded with an assertion (based on his defensive denial) that David's mother had been and was now fine. His father's protests notwithstanding, David's conversation with his father served to strengthen his understanding of his family system as not being normal.

The Myth of Restoration. Confrontation, more often than not, blows apart the myth of restoration as the adult child's expectations are disappointed. As the parent (or offender) responds in a manner congruent with past behavior, the hope of restoration looks like a pipe dream.

Rosa struggled with memories of cruel and malicious ritual abuse by her father. She asked her parents to come to one of her therapy sessions, which she used as an opportunity to confront them with her memories. The parents listened and responded with a relative degree of remorse. Her father, in particular, appeared stricken with fear by her words. Neither parent, in the presence of the care provider, denied Rosa's account of her childhood abuse. Rosa received a glimmer of hope that maybe she could reconcile her hatred toward her parents and find a restoration of a family she felt she had lost years before.

Several weeks later, Rosa's father stopped by Rosa's workplace with a package for her. He dropped it on her desk in silence and walked away. The package contained a volume of material from the False Memory Foundation, a group made up almost entirely of parents whose children have made allegations of childhood incest. The note with the material said, "Maybe the things you think you remember never really happened."

Rosa's smoldering hatred returned in full force. She knew at that moment that reconciliation with her family would not happen, that her dream of a family restored would not come to fruition. She let go of this hope with profound grief yet with a resolve to turn her energies and attention now to her new family, a supportive husband and an infant girl.

METHOD

Before confronting neglectful or abusive parents, building a foundation is advisable to cushion any distress from the process. Timing is important. The stage of confrontation in the recovery process follows an initial disclosure of the trauma history with a trusted professional, and a degree of developing understanding about the effects of the trauma on the adult self. Victim-survivors need to be coached to prepare themselves mentally and emotionally for the challenge of confrontation and to maintain control of the encounter as much as possible.

Mental Preparation

In preparing for the confrontation, the parishioner can rehearse the conversation ahead of time, in the form of letter writing or role-playing. Important questions to address are "What do I need to say?" and "What do I not want to say?"

Letter Writing. The letter-writing exercise puts thoughts and feelings into words, helping the parishioner organize what he or she would like to say. The pastoral caregiver can read the letter or listen as the careseeker reads the letter aloud, offering feedback and response. The letter is not meant to be sent; it is simply meant to focus the adult child's needs in regard to the encounter.

Role-Playing. Role-playing takes the form of the pastoral caregiver sitting in for the wounder as an actor in the confrontation. The careseeker is encouraged to say what she or he needs to say and then to share her or his feelings. The pastor might step out of the role long enough to coach, with suggestions such as, "Tell her how angry you are," or "What else do you need to say to him?"

Role-playing can be either a one-way exercise in which the adult child does the speaking, venting, and challenging without response, or a bilateral process in which the pastoral caregiver takes the part of responding as the wounder might. The caregiver, in the second instance, needs to be clued in ahead of time by the victim-survivor as to the wounder's personality and typical ways of relating.

What Needs to Be Said? Rehearsal or writing in response to the question "What do I need to say?" helps in pulling thoughts together and outlining points the survivor wants to make. Ideally this will be an encounter after which the victim-survivor feels she or he has said what needed to be said.

The careseeker can be coached to start the conversation by recalling a few moments from childhood for which she or he feels thankful toward the wounder. Mat wrote, in preparation for a confrontation with his alcoholic father, "You always provided well for us. I know how hard you worked, and I am grateful for that. Thank you for letting me take piano lessons, even when you thought it was a waste of time. You taught me the value of a dollar."

With this introduction done, the adult child then names the trauma, beginning with a general labeling of the dysfunction and moving to a more specific recalling of times when wounding occurred. Mat continued his letter with the following: "You are an alcoholic, Dad, and it has affected our whole family. I remember the Christmas you stumbled in drunk and knocked over the tree. I remember the time you lined up Mom and Billie and Susie and I, pointing your shotgun at us and threatening to kill us. I remember the times you and Mom fought all night, and I would fall asleep in school the next day because I hadn't gotten any sleep. I remember Billie and Susie and I hiding in the closet when you came home drunk. I remember as a teenager coming home drunk or stoned night after night and you not even noticing the difference."

The adult child also needs to focus on his or her feelings and can be coached to include this next in the letter or role-play. The focus should be on how the individual felt as a child. Mat wrote, "I missed you when you weren't around. I looked up to you, and didn't understand why you treated us the way you did. I often felt like you didn't love us. I was so hurt when you always broke your promise to take us to the movies or to the amusement park or to the beach. As a teenager I hated you. Here you were a counselor, and your son was falling apart and you didn't even notice."

Finally, the survivor can be encouraged to state what he or she would like from the offender in the present. This might include such desires as the wish for an apology, the need to hear the parent admit his or her abuse, or the longing to hear the parent say, "I love you."

Mat concluded his letter to his father with, "I wish you could see yourself through my eyes. I wish you knew how much you have damaged our lives. Will you ever admit to how you have hurt us? Will you ever say 'I'm sorry?' I know I can never get my childhood back, but one day I hope to have children of my own, and I pray you can be a healthy grandparent to them, even though you couldn't be a healthy father to me."

What Needs to Not Be Said? The survivor might be cautioned by the pastoral caregiver not to say or do anything that she or he might later regret, such as insulting or attacking the wounder, leaving in anger or hurt without saying all she needs to say, lying to make a point, threatening the parent, presenting an ultimatum, or intentionally hurting the abuser. The adult child needs to avoid encountering the offender in an aggressive or hostile manner. If the adult child feels aggressive or hostile in the preparation stage, then probably the timing is not right for a confrontation. The attitude of confrontation should be not vengeful but desirous of accountability.

When David confronted his mother about her depression, he met her smug denial of the severity of her problem. In frustration, he lied and told her that he had spoken with her doctor, Dr. Schultz, who agreed that his mother had a chronic mental illness. (Although David had indeed shared his concerns with Dr. Schultz, the doctor had made no comment on her mental health but had only listened to David's concerns.) The result of this confrontation was that David's mother stopped all visits to her doctor, and left David feeling guilt and responsibility for his mother's declining physical health.

Emotional Preparation. The parishioner can be coached ahead of time to expect that the wounder might be defensive, might deny the wounding, and might not be open to hearing the confrontation or to responding honestly. The adult survivor can expect to hurt even more after the encounter, yet this pain will diminish with processing and reintegration. For the confronter to be aware of the likelihood of a defensive response helps ready him or her for the confrontation.

Emotional expectations are best focused on the self rather than on the other person. For example, the adult child might hold expectations such as "I want to stop feeling responsible for my father's pain," "I just want to tell him that what he did wasn't okay," "I want to let her know that I remember those times, and that I've been hurt by it," or "I don't want to pretend anymore that everything's fine." Expectations such as "I want him to apologize," "I need her to understand what I'm feeling," or "I just want him to admit to what he did and to say that it was wrong" should be explored but recognized as out of the adult child's control. Expectations that depend on a certain response from the other should be minimized, whereas expectations that focus on the internal healing process of the individual should be sharpened.

Cindy (from the introduction) felt that to fully let go of the sibling incest, she needed to confront her brother about it. She wanted not to have to pretend around him anymore; she wanted to let him know how she had struggled with the intrapsychic results of the trauma, and she wanted to cleanse herself of shame, to "lay the accountability at his feet." In Cindy's case, the encounter had a positive result beyond her internal healing: Cindy's brother admitted to the abuse, expressing remorse and apology. He also disclosed to her that he had been sexually abused by one of their uncles when he was a small boy. The encounter with her brother helped Cindy move beyond her anger and shame, and Cindy became closer to her only sibling.

Controlling the Environment

The parishioner needs to control the setting for the confrontation as much as possible. This includes arranging the place, time, and attendance of the meeting.

Place. In planning the encounter, the victim-survivor needs to be encouraged to set up the confrontation on neutral and safe ground, rather than in the wounder's territory, particularly when the home of the offender was the place of the trauma.

Time. The parishioner should be coached to plan, at the outset, a time limit for the confrontation, rather than leaving the length of the encounter open-ended. Thirty minutes to an hour is usually adequate time. With the time-limited plan in place, the adult child has a boundary should the confrontation prove fruitless, hurtful, or off-track. Another meeting can always be arranged if the allotted time is too short.

Also important in controlling the time element is the selection of a time of day when the survivor is neither hungry nor tired. The adult child needs to be in his or her best form, as though prepared for an important examination or a ten-kilometer run.

Attendance. If a third party is present at the confrontation, it should be at the invitation of the adult child rather than of the offender. The survivor may feel safer and stronger with another person present or with a benevolent third party close by.

When Cindy confronted her brother, she chose to do it when her brother and his family were at her home for Thanksgiving dinner. After dessert, when her sister-in-law and nephew were clearing the table, Cindy asked her brother if he would like to go out for a walk (controlling the place). She knew a route that would take forty-five minutes (controlling the time). And although she wanted her conversation with her brother to be one-on-one, she had shared with her best friend her intention to confront him, asking if the friend would be available by phone later that evening if Cindy needed to call (controlling the attendance).

CONCLUSION

Healthy, considered confrontation serves as an agent of healing for the adult child. Differentiation, integration of value paradoxes, and demythology of the victim-survivor myths are all potential benefits to the survivor of childhood domestic trauma who has challenged the offender through direct confrontation.

The pastoral caregiver helps increase the potential growth resulting from the encounter through thoughtful and studied preparation with the adult child. The process of confrontation is a redemptive task, with the adult child gaining a new understanding of self, others, and God, as well as increased personal freedom for responsible participation in life.

chapter seven

Exorcising Internal Haunters

> "The one who should be going is you. I'm tired of your tormenting me. Leave me in peace once and for all!"
> "You will be condemned to hell for talking to me like this!"
> "No more than you!"
> "Shut your mouth! Who do you think you are?"
> "I know who I am! A person who has a perfect right to live her life as she pleases. Once and for all, leave me alone; I won't put up with you! I hate you, I've always hated you!"
> Tita had said the magic words that would make Mama Elena disappear forever. The imposing figure of her mother began to shrink until it became no more than a tiny light. As the ghost faded away, a sense of relief grew inside Tita's body.
> —Laura Esquivel, *Like Water for Chocolate*

When haunted internally by wounders from the past who can not be confronted face-to-face, the adult child needs to find other ways to challenge that offending presence. The confrontation is not unlike a ritual to exorcise the unwelcome haunter. As the ghosts fade away, a sense of relief grows for the victim-survivor. This chapter presents background and methods for indirectly confronting deceased wounders from the past or living figures with whom direct confrontation feels unsafe.

THEORY AND BACKGROUND

Many times a survivor of childhood trauma raises questions such as "Do I have to confront my perpetrator in order to heal?" "How can I ever resolve this anger toward my mother now that she's died?" or "I don't see how I can ever get past all this without facing my father, yet I really don't want to talk to him about it." The victim-survivor does not have to engage in person-to-person confrontation in order to heal. Resolution and integration are internal processes that are not conditional on external forgiveness or on making peace with the offender. The childhood myth holds out for restoration of the relationship with the wounder (as is described in chapter 4); yet although direct confrontation can certainly be helpful, it is not necessary to confront the historical source of the suffering in order to heal from childhood domestic trauma.

Interpersonal or Intrapsychic Confrontation?

Often the adult child either literally cannot confront figures from the past or—with good reason—simply does not want to confront the abuser directly. Often healing and recovery need to proceed without the process of direct confrontation with the wounder from the past. Many times an intrapsychic confrontation, rather than an interpersonal one, is the viable choice. In any of these situations, an indirect confrontation can adequately exorcise the internal haunters.

If Only He or She Were Alive. Many adult children turn for help after their perpetrators or wounders have died. Joan and Julie (introduced in chapter 5) were well into their fifties when they joined a group for adult children. Joan's father had died when she was a teen, and Julie's father had died shortly after the birth of her first child. Although they both expressed regret about not having the opportunity to confront their fathers, both were also determined to put the abuse to rest.

Other times, the offender is completely absent from the life of the victim-survivor, so confrontation is not a possibility. Kathy's parents had divorced when she was seven. She was haunted by flashbacks and nightmares of her father's sexual abuse of her from toddlerhood on up, yet she could not confront her father because she had no idea where he was. Her mother had not heard from him since he left. Kathy said, "It's as if he was dead. He may be dead for all I know. It would almost be easier if he was, because then I'd have the chance to tell him off at his grave and to lay this to rest once and for all."

The Suffering Offender. The offender may now be elderly or ill, or may be suffering from other conditions, so that in good conscience the adult child does not want to distress the person through pulling him or her into past injustices. The compassion, kindness, or integrity of the survivor hold him or her back from direct confrontation.

Ramon's aged mother resided in a nursing home. Although he longed to confront his mother with her complicity in his father's abuse, he felt it would be unfair to her to add the burden of accountability for the past to her day-to-day struggle with elderly life.

Out of Recovery. Not infrequently, the wounder is still chemically dependent, clearly emotionally unavailable, or psychically unsafe, making direct confrontation unrealistic or inappropriate. Jean's father still drank heavily. Even sober, he did not think clearly or act responsibly. Confrontation was out of the question for her.

Personal Choice. The victim-survivor may simply choose not to go the route of confrontation. This could be the case when the risk of losing the relationship, or of not being heard, is too threatening. Sometimes the willingness to engage face-to-face on emotional issues, or the trust to do so, is simply absent. There are times when the victim-survivor chooses to do the work of healing solely within the safe boundaries of the minister-parishioner relationship.

Sarah still lived with her now widowed mother. She had no desire to upset the balance they had forged with each other by bringing up pain from the past. She preferred to deal with her anger without person-to-person encounter.

Indirectly Challenging the Source

When face-to-face confrontation is not a viable option, the wounder can still be challenged through a number of intrapsychic techniques. A sense of justice for the adult child partly entails laying accountability for the wounding at the source of the trauma. The differentiation described in chapter 6, the catharsis, the spiritual development through enforcement of newly integrated value conflicts, and the demythologizing of victim-survivor myths all can result through indirectly challenging the source of the wounding as well as through direct confrontation.

Exorcism

Although the internal pain of the adult survivor may not be demonic, the adult child does battle figurative ghosts, haunters, and unwelcome forces within, metaphorical dybbuks that are able partially and intermittently to influence or dominate the thinking and behavior of the individual.

The Outside Source. The image of exorcism can be useful in several ways. First, it indicates that the source of the dis-ease with which the survivor struggles is outside the individual. The idea of possession in ancient belief has the effect of exonerating the individual from guilt or complicity. Although the victim-survivor needs to take responsibility for his or her life in the present, the accountability for past suffering lies with the offender.

Discharging Psychic Tension. The image of exorcism is also apt in that to exorcise entails bringing to the surface and discharging psychic tension. Figurative exorcism, as the indirect confrontation of childhood wounders, involves targeting, identifying, and alleviating unresolved conflict. The figurative exorcism results in a liberation of the spirit.

METHOD

Several methods are useful in the process of exorcising internal haunters: letter writing, guided imagery, empty-chair or role-playing techniques, and a well-planned visit to the gravesite of the offender.

Letter Writing

A letter to the offender, for self-healing rather than for sending, can serve the purpose of catharsis, clarification, and validation of feelings. The victim-survivor can be given guidelines for the letter writing, if he or she needs the structure. One simple outline follows the suggestions in chapter 6:

1. List several things from childhood about which you feel thankful toward the wounder.
2. Name the dysfunction.
3. List those things you needed from him or her but did not get.
4. Tell the offender how you felt then and how you feel now about the domestic trauma.

Many victim-survivors prefer to write a letter without structure or guidelines. The caregiver need only encourage the adult child to include details of the wounding, to express feelings of the hurt child, to vent anger toward the wounder, or to state other issues more specific to the individual parishioner.

The victim-survivor might also be encouraged to take on the role of the recipient of the letter and to write a letter back to herself or himself. This is most useful in situations where the wounding occurred through emotional unavailability of the caretaker due to multiple loss, family illness, or external demands on the family, rather than in situations of outright emotional, physical, or sexual abuse by the caretaker.

Guided Imagery

A guided meditation, with the minister as guide, can serve to bring the wounded child face-to-face with the wounder in a safe and protected setting. The guided meditation needs to include frequent reassuring phrases, which serve to contain the anxiety of the parishioner. These phrases might include "You are safe now," "You are strong," or "He can't hurt you now." The minister should, through the imagery, guide the parishioner into a relaxed state, a safe place, and then introduce the wounder into the environment.

The parishioner is given several minutes of silence to say what she or he needs to say and to ask the questions she or he needs to ask of the wounder. The caregiver encourages the adult child to focus on how she or he is feeling in the encounter. The victim-survivor is then given time to listen to how the offender responds, being guided to observe the interaction. The pastoral caregiver offers such guidance as, "Observe how he looks," "Notice the expression on her face," "How do you feel right now?" and "What is your physical self saying to you now?"

The pastoral guide can then encourage the parishioner to assert his or her newly developed strength. An example would be, "Tell him that he can't hurt you anymore. (Silence.) He has no power over you anymore. (Silence.) Tell him goodbye." The wounder is then exited from the guided meditation, and the parishioner guided to breathe in the security and nurturance of her or his safe place.

Finally, the adult child is guided to open her or his eyes when she or he feels ready. The parishioner is then affirmed for her or his strength and courage in facing the wounder, and the experience is processed together. (A written guided meditation is included as an appendix in this book.)

Guided imagery is not a useful technique for all adult survivors. Some will feel uncomfortable simply closing their eyes in the counseling setting. Others will be unable to focus on the meditation, being distracted by other thoughts and feelings. Still others will not want to give up the control necessary to be guided through a meditation.

Many adult children, however, experience a degree of healing and letting go through the guided imagery confrontation. Jennifer was surprised at her impulse to tell her deceased mother how much she loved her, even after venting feelings of rage and abandonment. She also experienced significant comfort from her mother's response: that she was sorry for everything, that she loved Jennifer, that she was at peace now, and that with all her heart she prayed for Jennifer's well-being.

Empty-Chair or Role-Playing Techniques

The third technique useful for intrapsychically confronting figures of the past is the empty-chair or role-playing technique. In this exercise, an empty chair is placed in the center of the room, and the parishioner is directed to speak to the chair as though the wounder is sitting in the chair. The parishioner is guided to say whatever comes to mind, however it sounds or feels, and to share feelings with the imagined wounder. The role of the minister in the empty-chair technique is to guide the parishioner with such suggestions as "Tell her how you felt about that," "Let him know how much you're hurting," or "Tell her how angry you've been."

Following the empty-chair confrontation, the parishioner is asked to sit in the empty chair and to speak back to herself or himself through the role of the wounder. Again, the caregiver can encourage honest, open sharing of feelings. Often through the role reversal, the parishioner is able to experience the wounder as more human and more caring than in past perception, thus enabling forgiveness and letting go. Other times, the reverse role-playing validates a perception of the wounder as intentionally hurtful. Either of these reverse role-playing results can be helpful in the integration of past experience and the subsequent healing of the wounded child. A variation on the empty-chair technique is a role-playing with the pastor acting the role of the offender, as described in chapter 6.

When Sarah practiced an empty-chair technique with her father (an incest perpetrator) in the empty chair, she tried to vent her rage at her father, only to curl into a ball and, in a child's voice, tell her father she didn't want him to leave her. Processing the encounter gave Sarah the opportunity to address the grief and sadness beneath her rage.

A Visit to the Gravesite

Finally, for those adult children whose offenders are deceased, a well-timed visit to the gravesite can be useful for exorcising internal haunters. The gravesite setting can trigger intense feeling in the survivor, to the extent that he or she allows it, and provide opportunity for considerable catharsis.

The cemetery is a setting for an encounter similar to the empty-chair exercise. Just as many who have lost one close to them go to the gravesite to talk to the deceased, so the adult child talks to the offender through words directed at the grave. Often the survivor has not been to the gravesite in ages; sometimes the site has not been visited since the burial.

This exercise can be planned in advance with the pastoral care provider, in a way similar to the preparation discussed in chapter 6 before a face-to-face confrontation with the offender. The careseeker is encouraged to voice memories, to vent anger, to share hurt and sadness, and to conclude with a message putting closure on the wound. The closure message might be "You can't hurt me anymore," "I'm going on with my life now," or "I'm leaving this pain with you, because I don't want to pass it on."

Following a lengthy pastoral counseling process in which she worked on healing from the verbal and emotional abuse of her alcoholic father, Nancy felt the need to visit his grave. For almost twenty years she had not been to the cemetery where he was buried. She described a period of tears when no words came, followed by the sharing of a flood of pent-up thoughts and memories. She told him how she had hated him as a child and how angry she was that he died before she could have a chance to resolve things with him.

Finally, Nancy spoke the exorcising words "I do not want to live with hatred in my heart anymore. I am letting you go, Daddy." She described feeling liberated as she left the cemetery.

CONCLUSION

Even a deceased or an absent parent can have a significant hold on the spirit of the survivor of childhood domestic trauma. The unresolved tension can leave the adult child feeling stuck, with the conflict from the legacy of dysfunction infecting the process of liberation. When direct confrontation is not an option, a figurative exorcising of the internal forces can occur, surfacing and discharging tension.

The differentiation, catharsis, integration of value conflicts, and demythologizing that result from indirectly challenging the offender free the careseeker for letting go and moving on, for recovering the lost child, and for restoring an immanent sense of the sacred (see chapters 8 and 9).

chapter eight

Recovering the Lost Child

How does one arrive somewhere when, without knowing it, one has always been there? How does it happen that confusion turns into clarity, fear of pain into freedom to experience feelings; that volumes of empty words turn into simple facts, the constant flight-from-self into being-with-oneself; that blindness turns into vision, deafness into hearing, indifference into empathy, ignorant crime into informed responsibility, murderous lusts into calm, clenched despair into relaxation, self-destruction into self-protection, self-alienation into self-harmony? None of this happens by an effort of will, by sermons, with the aid of theories, and least of all with the aid of medication. The effort of will can lead to even more clenched despair, moralizing to more effective denial, while medication and drugs can often lead to the causes of suffering remaining forever unknowable, the keys to the truth forever undiscoverable.

—Alice Miller, *For Your Own Good*

As the victim-survivor moves through a process of sharing the story, demythologizing, integrating spiritual values, and confronting wounders of the past, the individual faces a well of grief over his or her lost childhood. As previously held defenses are let down, the overwhelming sense of loss rings clear. The childhood years are years that the victim-survivor can never get back.

Important in the step of moving beyond the wounding is the process of recovering the lost child. Although the years cannot be gotten back and the trauma cannot be reversed, the adult child is capable of recovering a degree of the receptive, wide-eyed wonder and trust that mark early childhood.

Recovering the lost child entails finding and embracing the part of oneself that has frozen in time, the part that still feels like a three- or four-, seven- or eight-, or eleven-year-old, which has hoped against hope to be loved, rescued, understood, or valued. Alice Miller answers the rhetorical questions of the epigraph by stressing that to arrive at that place of wholeness requires feeling empathy for the childhood pain and discovering the childhood needs.

THEORY AND BACKGROUND

The victim-survivor needs to make peace with that child within him or her, and must learn to love and to parent that child within, in order to be finally released from the dysfunctional legacy. Bernie Siegel writes that "only through loving the child within us can we insure that love will be the legacy we leave for our children. Otherwise we will pass on the pain we still feel, the needs that were never met, just as our parents passed theirs on to us, and their parents before them *ad infinitum*."[1]

Much recovery literature refers to the "inner child" as the internalization of the historical child in the still-developing self of the adult. "Inner child" describes that part of oneself that represents the feelings and personhood of the historical child. Often the inner child of the victim-survivor still carries the pain, anxiety, sadness, and suffering that the individual carried in the past, along with the resultant self-image and beliefs about God, others, and the world. The survivor of childhood domestic trauma has the challenge of loving the child, tending the child's wounds, and liberating the child to that receptive, wide-eyed wonder.

Loving the Child

Mat, having completed significant work in recovery from his growing up with an alcoholic father, remarked one day about his best friend's relationship with his four-year-old son. His best friend was crazy about his son. "You know," Mat said, "I almost envy Billy. I never had anyone who was crazy about me.

"All children," Mat concluded, "should have someone who is crazy about them."

Chapter 4 addressed the task of connecting with the historical child as a means of demythologizing. Faced with building new sacred stories beyond the myths of childhood, the adult child still carries the sense of having been unloved, unwanted, neglected, or abused, and now faces the reality that the needs for love, understanding, closeness, and affection will not be met by the original caretakers. Beyond connecting with the historical child, the survivor of childhood wounding needs to find the means to love that child and to become crazy about that child. Understanding that loving, healthy parenting is not going to come from the source of the wounding, the adult child learns to meet the need to be cared for by becoming a parent to himself or herself.

Tending the Child Within

In meeting the child within, the victim-survivor needs to respond to pain with compassion, to guilt with forgiveness and grace, to sadness with comfort, to loneliness with presence, to despair with hope, and to anger with righteous indignation at the reality of injustice. The adult child faces the task of tending the historical child's wounds.

Survivors of childhood wounding often refer in pejorative and critical terms to the historical child they once were. John, when talking about himself as a child, always used the word "pathetic." A fierce advocate of the rights of children, John would never use this word to describe any other child. By pathetic, he said he meant forlorn, lost, and needy. Anita often described herself, in the early childhood years before her parents divorced, as a "brat." She too respected and enjoyed children, and would seldom use a derogatory term to describe any child other than the child she had been. By brat, Anita said she meant that she made her needs known and that she always wanted to be the center of attention.

Both John and Anita needed to tend the children whom they were, to feel empathy for the pain of those children, and to respond with unburdened caregiving. To fully release themselves from the bonds of the dysfunctional past and to experience themselves in the present as whole and worthy of grace, adult children need to tend the child within. The victim-survivor who thinks he was a pathetic child, who thinks she was a brat, who feels disgust or pity when reflecting about the child he was, or who feels shame or self-conscious distress upon remembering herself when young, will also tend to hold a negative self-image of himself or herself as an adult. The child within needs healthy, respectful caretaking. "For the human spirit is virtually indestructible, and its ability to rise from the ashes remains as long as the body draws breath," Miller writes.[2] Meeting with and tending the inner child constitute a rising from the ashes for the spirit of the adult child.

Receptive, Wide-Eyed Wonder

"Only children can hear the song of the male house mouse," writes Annie Dillard.

> Only children keep their eyes open. The only thing they have got is sense; they have highly developed "input systems," admitting all data indiscriminately. Matt Spireng has collected thousands of arrowheads and spearheads; he says that if you really want to find arrowheads, you must walk with a child—a child will pick up everything.[3]

The healthy young child is open to learning in each moment, whether in a preschool classroom, at the river's edge, or under the kitchen table. The healthy young child is keenly responsive to the people, animals, and things in her or his world, whether a revered parent, a strange child at the playground, a garden toad, or a wooden train. The healthy young child is eager for new experience, eager to try new things and to develop new skills. With age, all lose a degree of the openness, responsiveness, and eagerness of the young child. Yet the adult child of a dysfunctional family has aged prematurely, has lost a degree of the openness, responsiveness, and eagerness of the young child before the natural course of time. Many adult children say, "I feel like I never got a chance to be a child," or "I feel like I had to grow up too quickly."

In recovering the lost child, the survivor of childhood wounding experiences a thawing of his or her frozen soul, remembers how to ask questions and how to listen to the asking, restores the openness to learn from the ordinary, and again "hear[s] the song of the male house mouse." The survivor exchanges bitterness, cynicism, and ardent mistrust for a measure of open, wide-eyed innocence. The survivor exchanges some of the stoic sense of overresponsibility and some of the need always to do things right for a taste of mischievousness and a thirst for new experience.

METHOD

The spirit of the child thrives on growing, on the learning of things mysterious, and on receiving grace. To recover the lost child is to find the keys to the dominion of God, to unlock the spirit of life that makes body and soul alive in love: "Let the little children come to me, and do not stop them; for it is to such as these that the kingdom of God belongs. Truly I tell you, whoever does not receive the kingdom of God as a little child will never enter it" (Luke 18:16b-17).

The pastoral caregiver is able to help the victim-survivor recover the lost child through support and encouragement and through the use of several methods in guiding the parishioner to love the child within, to tend the child within, and to thaw out the open, wide-eyed wonder of childhood.

Loving the Child Within

"When I think of who I was as a little girl," wrote Judy in her journal, "I feel a lot of sadness. I used to spin elaborate fantasies about how my biological mother would come and find me and take me home with her and really love me. I deserved to be loved, and I knew that even then.

"I think my mom probably did love me, but she just didn't know how to show it. She commented the other day on how much my sister *holds* the new baby. She thought it so unusual! Did she hold me as a baby? I can't remember a time when she held me in her lap.

"Who held me as a newborn? My mom says I was in a foster home until they got me when I was three months old. I wonder if they held me in that foster home. I'm shaking and crying just thinking about it."

The pastoral caregiver needs to help the adult child find ways to give himself or herself the unconditional love that his or her parents were unable to provide when he or she was a child. Several techniques can be useful.

A Letter to the Child. A simple exercise for expressing love to the inner child is a letter-writing exercise. The adult child pictures himself or herself at a certain age, perhaps at an age when the child was feeling particularly alone or wounded. The victim-survivor then writes a letter to this child, a letter of love. The parishioner might share feelings of esteem for the child's courage and strength in bearing the trauma, praise for the child's accomplishments (which have gone unnoticed by the family), or appreciation for the child's temperament. The letter might also share words of sorrow and empathy for the pain the child has had to endure, words of righteous anger for the injustice the child has been victim to, and words of encouragement, wisdom, or inspiration to the child for facing what lies ahead. Finally, the letter should share the love and affection that the adult feels for the child, and a vow of loyalty.

On the Occasion of One's Birth. Judy's church had a custom of asking godparents of baptized babies to write a letter to the baby "on the occasion of your baptism." The letter was given to the parents, to be opened by the child on the day of her or his confirmation. Judy was inspired by this tradition to write a letter to herself as a newborn "on the occasion of your birth." She wrote how perfect she was, how precious she was in God's sight, and what a gift she was. She welcomed herself to the world with love. Judy signed the letter, "Your guardian angel."

Few adult children think they were not lovable and precious as a baby. It can be helpful for the victim-survivor to imagine what he or she was like as a newborn and to write a letter to that newborn "on the occasion of your birth." This exercise can bring out immense feelings of love for the inner child and a recognition that all children are gifts from God.

Guided Imagery. For those who respond well to this technique, guided imagery is also useful for loving the child within. The parishioner, with eyes closed, is guided into a state of relaxation by the pastoral caregiver through deep breathing and conscious relaxation of each part of the body. Next the parishioner is taken back in time to an age when he or she was hurting and needed love. The adult takes time to experience this child, noting the child's appearance, what the child seems to be feeling, and what the adult experiences in observing the child. Next the adult converses with the child, telling him or her what needs to be said and listening to what needs to be heard. (The pastoral caregiver can guide the conversation to focus on feelings.)

Finally, the adult tells the child how loved the child is and that, when the child needs him or her, simply to ask. Following an embrace or a period of holding the child on the lap, the parishioner is guided by the caregiver to say goodbye, to leave the past, to reenter the present, and to return to the room. The exercise is then processed and the parishioner encouraged to return to the exercise in his or her own time. (The appendix includes a written guided meditation for recovering the child within.)

Tending the Child Within

In a poem called "Can't Sleep," Mildred wrote of the battle between the pain of the child within and the impulse of her adult self to squelch the child's claims on her energy:

> Optimism is gone
> Reality stands stark
> Pain, anger, despair

> Who am I
> Why am I
> How do I find out?
> The child screams "help."
> The grownup says "be still."
> Running away solves the moment
> Work and fatigue soak up the hours.
> The merry-go-round never stops
> The brass ring is called Tuesday.

"Tuesday" refers to Mildred's Tuesday-night group for adult children of dysfunctional families, where Mildred addressed the child's pain and responded to the child's demands by opening up to others about the feelings of her inner child and by talking with others about ways to meet the inner child's needs. Mildred's poetry became a way of tending the inner child, as the words expressed feeling and the verses spoke passion.

The minister in pastoral care with the survivor of childhood abuse works with the survivor to develop ways to tend the inner child. These might include physical activities (such as swimming, in-line skating, or playing in a softball league), social activities (such as joining a men's or women's chorus, trying out for the local community theater, taking a Chinese cooking class, or working with a nonprofit organization), spiritual activities (such as practicing meditation, keeping a journal, writing poetry, or worshiping at the local temple), and leisure activities (such as going to the movies, walking in the woods, or reading a good book).

The activities need to be custom-designed to address needs and wishes the inner child holds. Activities that are passive, reckless, compulsive, or unhealthy need to be discouraged, as these activities do not tend the inner child but thwart the child through responding dysfunctionally to feelings. Activities such as spending the evening in front of the television, eating a pint of chocolate ice cream, "buying myself something," "kicking back with a couple of cold ones," or sleeping until noon would usually not be in the best interest of a child.

Many survivors of childhood wounding have not learned the value of taking care of themselves in simple ways. The survivor who is stressed out will not automatically think of simplifying her or his daily routine; the adult child who is worn-out will not necessarily decide to get to bed earlier; the victim-survivor who is fatigued will not regularly be concerned with eating more nutritionally. Tending to the needs of the child includes getting enough rest, eating nutritional meals, and scheduling one's day sensibly.

Open, Wide-Eyed Wonder. One week, Mildred splashed in puddles following a late afternoon rain. Another week she took herself to a penny arcade on the beach, the former site of an amusement park to which her alcoholic father had often promised to take her (a promise he never fulfilled). She cherished the moments when she let out her inner child, relishing these moments as a parent relishes special times with a young child.

The pastoral caregiver can encourage the survivor of childhood trauma to be a child sometimes, to do things as an adult that he or she was not able to do as a child, and simply to "have fun." The adult child often takes himself or herself too seriously and has difficulty having fun. Recovering the child within entails learning again how to make the most of each moment.

Alternative approaches to the traditional verbal pastoral care model can be quite helpful for the adult survivor to retrieve a measure of the open, wide-eyed wonder of childhood. Art, music, movement, and creative writing are all helpful in tapping the creativity, expressiveness, responsiveness, and openness of the inner child.

Art. Drawing, painting, and working with clay are useful for the parishioner to create representations of the inner life. Pastoral suggestions such as "Draw a picture of your family," "Paint your sadness," or "Use the clay to make a sculpture of your anger" can elicit powerful artistic responses from the inner child.

Cynthia (from the introduction) was asked to draw a picture of her anger. With crayons she drew big black marks on the paper, filling the center of the page with forceful, determined scribbles.

She followed this by coloring over the angry black marks to make a flying diamond-shaped black kite with two brightly colored bows on its tail. She interpreted the drawing as meaning that her anger was not necessarily a bad thing but could be transformed (the kite) and utilized for empowerment (flying).

Music. "David took the lyre and played it with his hand, and Saul would be relieved and feel better, and the evil spirit would depart from him" (1 Sam. 16:23b). The survivor of childhood domestic trauma can be encouraged to listen to favorite passages of music, to sing, to play an instrument, to write songs, or to try a hand at percussion rhythm as a way to connect with the inner child and to move toward liberation from the wounding. Music expresses and represents a range of emotions, values, and aspirations. Either listening to or making music can be a healing art.

Sarah collected a number of folk songs from various artists and compiled a tape of her favorites. The lyrics from one of the songs especially struck a chord in her: the image of a girl swinging on a swing, persisting in being a little child in spite of the abuse of her home. Her inner child, Sarah said, liked to listen to that song because she had often dissociated from the trauma of her home by looking out the window and imagining herself swinging. Sarah also included on her tape the Winnie the Pooh theme song, because Pooh had helped her hold on to her childhood a bit longer than she might have without him. Sarah turned to this tape often during times of shame, loneliness, or sadness about her lost childhood. She found considerable comfort and restoration in the music.

Movement. The pastoral caregiver can guide the adult child to use movement or expressive dance as a channel for releasing the spontaneity and vigor of the inner child. Expressive dance serves to stimulate, enliven, restore, and free the participant.

One exercise of expressive dance that may be helpful for the victim-survivor is for the careseeker to choose a meaningful passage of scripture (a length of several verses) and "choreograph" the passage. For example, the careseeker might choose Isaiah 40:31:

> Those who wait for the Lord shall renew their strength,
> > they shall mount up with wings like eagles,
> they shall run and not be weary,
> > they shall walk and not faint.

With a passage such as this, the parishioner can be given the assignment of expressing each phrase of the passage through an interpretive movement and piecing the movements together to make a coherent dance. This exercise works well in small group settings: members pair up to choreograph one phrase each, then pairs teach the whole group the movement for consecutive verses, until the group has learned together an expressive dance for the entire passage.

Creative Writing. "The pen," writes Thomas Moore, "expressing the soul's passion, is mightier than the sword because the imagination can change the life of a people at their very roots."[4] Many victim-survivors of childhood wounding use creative writing to recover the lost child, with good results. Poetry and story writing can sensitize the adult child to the historical child, can unify what feels like broken pieces of childhood, and can channel the experience of the child into redemptive, validating expression.

Carlos was devastated by the suicide of his father in his early teens. In adulthood, he wrote the following cathartic verse describing the moment he learned of his father's death:

> An unexpected shock of fact,
> Hits with careful, piercing, aim.
> The buzzard's beak, not knowing tact,
> In wretched hunger takes the game.

Jennifer, drawing on autobiographical experience, wrote a poignant short story of a young woman remembering childhood abuse. "What did I do to deserve this treatment?" a paragraph read.

> I walk quietly around the house, my mannerisms hesitant, like an unwelcome visitor in somebody else's home. I try so hard to be per-

fect, flawless, and pure, but every day he lets me know that I am not his angel. Everything is my fault. The dog barks, "sorry, daddy." I spill my milk accidentally and I can see the fire in his eyes, "sorry, daddy." The volume on the television set is too damn loud, "sorry, daddy." I'm sorry; I'm really sorry; I'm so sorry. Please forgive me. I need you. Please don't hate me. I love you. My apologies echo in my mind. Will it ever be his turn to apologize to me?

Parenting

Often adult children describe an experience of healing childhood wounds through positive parenting of their own children. Many victim-survivors in recovery experience a sense of restoring their own lost childhood through actively participating in the childhood of their offspring.

Although much has been written about the risk of passing on dysfunction from one generation to the next, and although passing on the pain tends to be one of the worst fears of the survivor of childhood domestic trauma, it is also true that the adult child who has been able to end the cycle of dysfunction can find immense joy and healing in fostering the growth and wholeness of her or his own children.

CONCLUSION

Robert Coles's description of the intimate interweaving of the psychological and spiritual lives of children offers solid argument for work on recovery of the lost child:

> As I go over the interviews I've done with children, I find certain psychological themes recurring. I hear children (on tape) talking about their desires, their ambitions, their hopes, and also their worries, their fears, their moments of deep and terrible despair--all connected in idiosyncratic ways, sometimes, with Biblical stories, or with religiously sanctioned notions of right and wrong, or with rituals such as prayer or meditation. Indeed, the entire range of children's

mental life can and does connect with their religious and spiritual thinking.[5]

Recovery of the lost child brings the victim-survivor home to the roots of her or his own spirituality. The pastoral caregiver, in guiding and encouraging this process, facilitates the careseeker's developing spiritual clarity, finding optimistic vision, and arriving at an informed sense of responsibility.

chapter nine

Restoring the Sacred

> "You wondered if original sin might not have something to do with repeating our parents' mistakes. That struck me.
> "I am finally understanding just the tip of the iceberg about what Resurrection means," Daddy was saying to Adrian. "I'm talking about the Resurrection as it applies to each of us. It means coming up through what you were born into, then understanding objectively the people your parents were, and how they influenced you. Then finding out who you are, in terms of how you carry forward what they put in you, and how your circumstances have shaped you. And then . . . and then . . . now here's the hard part! And then you have to slough off your 'original sin,' in the sense you defined it, Adrian. You have to go on to find out what you are in the human drama, or body of God. The what beyond the who, so to speak."
>
> —Gail Godwin, *Father Melancholy's Daughter*

The process of restoring the spirit of the victim-survivor has been set in motion and fueled through integrating value paradoxes, challenging victim-survivor myths, breaking the silence, confronting the dysfunction, and recovering the lost child. The final work of restoration entails passing beyond the suffering of the past and moving toward becoming a center of freedom and love (or, as Gail Godwin phrases it in the epigraph, finding out "what [one is] in the human drama, or body of God"). This process is one of restoring the sacred in the immanent world of the survivor of childhood domestic trauma.

THEORY AND BACKGROUND

Having come to terms with the trauma of the past, the adult child faces the monumental (yet grace-filled) task of reflecting the image of God in being and becoming. Having been freed for whole and responsible engagement with life, the adult child is called to find his or her place in the divine-human drama: to restore a hope grounded in religious tradition, to tap into the mystery of the holy, and to develop a religious response to a world in which domestic trauma is a reality.

Toward a New Eschatological Hope

Restoration, for the wounded adult child, is a reconciliation as much with the future as with the past, as the survivor reclaims health and breaks away from the cycle of wounding behavior. The restoration can be understood as a multigenerational restoration, as the adult child sloughs off the "original sin" of repeating the mistakes of her or his ancestors.

The survivor of childhood wounding has an unstoppable capacity for hope. As is discussed in previous chapters, many adult children have held on to a dream of reconciliation with those from whom they have been estranged, a dream that one day things will be all right and the family will be restored. The victim-survivor has held on to a conditional hope: "If only I can say it right to my mother to make her understand"; "If only my father would be open to hearing when I talk to him"; "If only trust is there and the spirit is working and grace enters in, we can make this better"; "If only my father would say he's sorry"; "If only my mother could say she loved me"; "If only our family could really talk together, shed tears for the past and the losses." And so on. Although the adult child is often encouraged in this sort of hope through the church (backed by secular scripture), more often than not this is a vain hope. For the adult child in recovery, reconciliation and restoration mean something quite different from this distorted eschatological dream.

Most often for the adult child, healing the wound means letting go of the secular hope and transforming the mythological hope into a hope grounded in the power of the sacred in the midst of human suffering. To fully make use of his or her unstoppable capacity for hope, the adult child needs to move beyond the longing for love from unloving family members, to transcend the hunger for something more from others, to grow past the belief in an external rescuer, and to let go of the expectation of someone paying a price for what has been done.

Through letting go, the survivor voices a resounding no to the continuing cycle of dysfunction, with a hope of liberation for living with a degree of life choice, with a sense of responsibility for oneself, and with a proficiency to love and be loved. Reconciliation with the sacred for the adult child involves growing beyond the dysfunctional dynamic and passing on a model of domestic wholeness, not domestic dysfunction, to future generations. Free from this "original sin," the victim-survivor can confidently expect to bequeath not the legacy of unnecessary trauma to her or his community, but a model of the authentic suffering servant, the wounded yet redeemed healer.

Close to the heart of the Jewish faith is trust in Yahweh, who is ever faithful to the divine-human covenant. The covenant does not negate tragedy, injustice, and suffering within the community; rather, the covenant promises God's faithful presence in the midst of the pain. God does not abandon or desert God's people; hope lies in God's unending presence:

> Have you not known? Have you not heard?
> The Lord is the everlasting God,
>   the Creator of the ends of the earth.
> He does not faint or grow weary;
>   his understanding is unsearchable.
> He gives power to the faint,
>   and strengthens the powerless.
>
> . . . .
>
> Those who wait for the Lord shall renew their strength,
>   they shall mount up with wings like eagles,

> they shall run and not be weary,
>> they shall walk and not faint. (Isa. 40:28-31)

The Christian hope lies in a Savior who, far from erasing suffering and injustice from the lives of his followers, enters into the suffering and injustice of the world with an incarnational promise of redemption. Christ suffers and dies with his followers, sharing through his presence an immanent experience of the divine in the midst of brokenness: "We are afflicted in every way, but not crushed; perplexed, but not driven to despair; persecuted, but not forsaken; struck down, but not destroyed; always carrying in the body the death of Jesus, so that the life of Jesus may also be made visible in our bodies" (2 Cor. 4:8).

Victim-Survivor Myths Revisited

When Peter reported experiencing an unexpected and startling expression of love from his mother, a friend replied to him, "That sounds like grace." Peter deliberated on this pronouncement, feeling slightly troubled by it. As he spoke about it with his pastor, Peter concluded, "Grace isn't a bad thing, is it?" Peter had grown up connecting grace with sin, so the word "grace" triggered thoughts of being judged, falling short, and feeling worthless. His reflection about grace brought him to the realization that it was not he who fell short, it was his theology that fell short.

The pastoral care process leads the parishioner to tap into the mystery of the holy and to come up with new and surprising awarenesses. Having experienced, through healing from childhood wounding, the divine power to renew and transform human life and to redeem human suffering, the parishioner is freed to integrate new sacred stories into her or his being and becoming. Annie Dillard writes:

> Cruelty is a mystery and the waste of pain. But if we describe a world to compass these things, a world that is a long, brute game, then we bump against another mystery: the inrush of power and light, the

canary that sings on the skull. Unless all ages and races of [people] have been deluded by the same mass hypnotist (who?), there seems to be such a thing as beauty, a grace wholly gratuitous.[1]

Freed from the dysfunctional victim-survivor mythology, the parishioner faces the call to develop a functional theology, to embrace grace as well as judgment, justice as well as oppression, and "the inrush of power and light" as well as the reality of cruelty.

In the recovery process, the victim-survivor myths become transformed into sacred stories encompassing a divine hope grounded in religious tradition. The myth of the good parent might be transformed into a sacred story encompassing the image of the good shepherd. The myth of control might be transformed into a sacred story encompassing the wisdom that for everything there is a season and a time for every purpose under heaven. The savior myth might be transformed into a sacred story encompassing the suffering savior who does not rescue yet brings hope for resurrection. The myth of normalcy might be transformed into a sacred story encompassing the promise that the old has passed away and the new has come. The myth of restoration might be transformed into a sacred story encompassing the singing of God's song in a strange land.

Whole People Heal People

Domestic dysfunction usually has been set into motion generations ago and passed on by ancestor after ancestor who violated his or her partner and wounded his or her offspring (who in turn passed on the abuse to their partners and offspring). As descendants reeled from the pain, denied or avoided the reality of the damage, ran blindly from the demons chasing them, and drowned the hurt with alcohol, sexual acting out, or aggression, they added their own unique dysfunction to the original sin and passed on the pain, along with the responsibility for reconciliation, to succeeding generations.

Restoration is a process that resolves the insidious cycle of dysfunction. Restoration puts closure on the "sins of the fathers" (and mothers), paying the debt once and for all by wrestling the demon of suffering to the ground and coming up victorious. Restoration builds hope grounded in redemptive experience and restores a positive alliance with the future.

Deborah found meaning in a phrase that caught her attention at an ALANON group: "Hurt people hurt people." To this motif she added a parallel truth: "Whole people heal people." A religious response to a world in which domestic trauma is a reality is a response of striving to meet human suffering with compassion, and human guilt with grace. One is freed for this response through transforming the pain and the drama of the childhood wounding. The parishioner needs to move beyond her or his identity as a victim, a survivor, or an adult child of a dysfunctional family, and into an identity as a child of God, broken yet redeemed. In this identity the parishioner experiences a deep solidarity with the whole of suffering creation.

METHOD

Perhaps the most critical pastoral function in working with the survivor of childhood domestic trauma is nurturing the restoration of the sacred within the parishioner. The pastoral caregiver represents gracious relationship, communicating the unconditional, all-encompassing, empowering love of God for the adult child. Pastoral care is grounded in trust in the divine power to liberate, to redeem, and to make new the life of the wounded. The caregiver communicates confident, unbending trust in this divine power and in the hope for restoration within the parishioner. The pastoral caregiver respects and responds to the spirit of the victim-survivor: to her intelligence, to his affective life, to her self-consciousness, to his capacity to relate to others, to her sense of freedom and responsibility. In nurturing the restoration of the sacred within the adult child, the pastoral caregiver uses several avenues, including sacred story, ritual, spiritual guidance, and giving back to the community.

Developing New Sacred Stories

Many survivors of childhood wounding hold the conviction that they could not have survived childhood without God's help, or that they could not have persevered through the recovery without God's strength. Many attribute the healing process and the hope for wholeness to the divine, expressing a feeling that with God lies credit for the growth.

As the parishioner works toward a new mythology, a functional theology that does not deny the wounding yet does redeem the suffering, the pastoral caregiver guides the parishioner into an integration that is personal and true to the experience of the individual. The examples earlier in this chapter of transformation of victim-survivor myths into sacred stories are intended simply as examples, not as suggested substitute myths for the parishioner. The parishioner needs to come to his or her own integrated theology. The pastoral caregiver can help through offering appropriate scripture passages or readings, through dialoguing and challenging, and through honest sharing of his or her own deeply felt sacred stories.

Suggested scriptures for each myth in transformation include the following passages.

Transforming the Myth of the Good Parent
    Isaiah 26:3–4 ("Trust in the Lord forever.")
    Psalm 23 ("The Lord is my shepherd.")
    Psalm 91 (refuge under God's wings)
    John 10:11–17 (Jesus the Good Shepherd)
    Romans 8 (Nothing can separate us from God's love.)

Transforming the Myth of Control
    Psalm 91 (refuge under God's wings)
    Ecclesiastes 3:1–11a ("For everything there is a season.")
    Luke 12:22–31 ("Consider the lilies.")
    1 Corinthians 13:11–13 ("Now we see in a mirror, dimly.")
    Revelation 21:1–5 ("a new heaven and a new earth")

Transforming the Savior Myth
    Psalm 27 ("The Lord is the stronghold of my life.")
    Isaiah 53 (a man of sorrow, acquainted with grief)
    Luke 1:67–80 (Zechariah's prophecy: "light to those who sit in darkness")
    2 Corinthians 1:3–5 (God comforts us in affliction.)
    Colossians 1:11–29 ("May you be made strong with all . . . strength.")

Transforming the Myth of Normalcy
    Psalm 138 (God will fulfill God's purpose for me.)
    Joel 2:28–29 ("I will pour out my spirit on all flesh.")
    2 Corinthians 4:1–13 ("treasure in clay jars")
    Romans 5:1–5 ("We are justified by faith.")
    Romans 8:1–2, 15 ("no condemnation for those who are in Christ Jesus")

Transforming the Myth of Restoration
    Isaiah 35 (restoration of all that is broken)
    Isaiah 43:1–3a, 18–19, 25 ("Do not fear, for I have redeemed you.")
    Isaiah 61:1–3a (good news of deliverance)
    John 16:21–22 ("When a woman is in labor, she has pain.")
    John 14:18–27 ("I will not leave you orphaned; I am coming to you.")

Using Ritual: Healing Services

Development of sacred stories is one important source for spiritual growth and development. Another source is healing ritual. The parishioner can experience significant release from wounding of the past, as well as considerable hope, from a healing service. The pastoral caregiver can either lead a healing service or refer the parishioner to a healing service in another location. The introduction to the healing services and prayers in the *United Methodist Book of Worship* reads:

> God does not promise that we shall be spared suffering but does promise to be with us in our suffering. Trusting that promise, we are enabled to recognize God's sustaining presence in pain ... and estrangement. A Service of Healing is not necessarily a service of curing, but it provides an atmosphere in which healing can happen. The greatest healing of all is the reunion or reconciliation of a human being with God. When this happens, physical healing sometimes occurs, mental and emotional balance is often restored, spiritual health is enhanced, and relationships are healed. For the Christian the basic purpose of spiritual healing is to renew and strengthen one's relationship with the living Christ.[2]

Jean participated in a healing service at an Anglican church that used a "Healing of Ancestry" liturgy. With other participants, she named in her heart those in her ancestry for whom she prayed for wholeness and from whom she prayed for release. The liturgy aimed at healing ancestral wounds. Jean found the service moving and hopeful. She experienced through the service a measure of forgiveness toward her ancestors (as she prayed for her parents and grandparents), a degree of letting go (as she offered to God's mercy the past pain of the family), and a movement toward restoration of her spirit (as she prayed for release from the heritage of sin).

A healing service usually incorporates the tradition of the laying on of hands, with words such as, "May the power of God's indwelling presence heal you of all illnesses—of body, mind, spirit, and relationships—that you may serve God with a loving heart. Amen."[3]

Doug, a victim of childhood physical abuse by his father, wrote his own healing liturgy for abuse survivors. Through the writing, he formulated a developing awareness of the immanence of the sacred, even in—indeed, especially in—suffering. As he shared the healing service with trusted friends, he experienced affirmation and confirmation of the liturgically expressed hope.

Reacquainting Oneself with God

In restoring the sacred within, the pastoral caregiver functions as spiritual director, praying for her or his directees and guiding the parishioner in spiritual exercises designed to help the individual become more intimately acquainted with the holy in her or his life. Appropriate spiritual exercises include guided meditation and letter writing.

Guided Meditation. Guided meditation can be used to bring the individual into conscious union with his or her understanding of the holy. As with other guided imagery exercises, this one begins with the parishioner closing her or his eyes and attaining a state of relaxation, through the suggestions of the caregiver. The parishioner is guided to breathe in peace and breathe out tension. The parishioner is next asked to travel to a safe place and to drink in the serenity of that place. Then the holy is introduced into the safe place, in the form of a "wise person" or a dove or other animal, or simply in an aural form. The parishioner "listens" to the holy, converses with the holy, observes and experiences the holy. The caregiver encourages the parishioner to pay attention to feelings, thoughts, senses, and observations about the other.

Finally, the careseeker is guided to ask the holy being one question and to listen for the answer. The careseeker thanks the holy being, and the holy being invites the individual to return anytime. Then the careseeker says goodbye and takes leave of the sacred place, returning to the pastoral care setting and opening his or her eyes. Following the guided imagery exercise, the pastor and parishioner process the experience.

The caregiver can use the preceding guidelines in designing a guided meditation that is appropriate to the individual, or she or he may use the written guided meditation that appears in the appendix. An alternative meditation for restoring the sacred within is Howard Clinebell's "cupped-hand exercise," a guided imagery that involves releasing guilt, tension, and a sense of burden, and taking in the healing Spirit of Life. This meditation follows:

> Close your eyes, put your hands out in front to form a bowl. Imagine that you are putting into your hands the feelings and fears that you're holding onto and would like to let go of. These feelings can

> relate to your grief or anything else. [Pause.]
>
> Now, reach out as far as you can, and turn your hands over, turning over what's in your hands to the Spirit of the Universe. Let go of it.... Now sit quietly for a few minutes. [Pause.]
>
> Form the bowl a second time. Imagine this time it's a receptor. Let the energy of the Spirit of Life present in this room, at this moment, the energy of the love of God flow through your hands like a stream of healing light. Let it flow up through your arms and throughout your whole body. Feel the flow of life energy.[4]

Judy felt tremendous relief and a sense of grace in doing this exercise. She said she often repeats the exercise at home when she feels she is losing touch with the sacred.

Letters to and from God. Another exercise in spiritual direction that the pastoral caregiver can draw upon in working with the parishioner to restore the sacred within is a letter-writing technique. Initially, the individual is asked to write a letter to God, a form of prayer including emotions of the moment, unresolved conflict, longings, and feelings toward and about God. This letter can be shared with the pastor, who offers dialogue concerning the contents of the letter.

Second, the individual is asked to write a letter to himself or herself from God. As an exercise in listening to the holy, the careseeker writes from God's point of view. Often this exercise helps the individual personally experience what he or she knows to be true of God's comprehensive, unconditional, and empowering love. The parishioner not infrequently experiences an element of surprise and appreciation in immersing himself or herself in this way in God's love. As an added twist, the individual can give the letter to the pastor, to be mailed to her or him at a later date. The receiving of the letter reinforces and validates the initial experience of the gracious love of the holy.

It should be noted that every now and then, an individual writes a judging, guilt-inducing letter from God. The judgmental letter should be processed, with the pastoral caregiver sharing a different experience of God and inquiring about what happened to the love and grace of God in the letter. It goes without saying that the judgmental letter should not be mailed at a later date. The parishioner does not need to experience the condemnation twice.

Prayer. Occasionally the victim-survivor of childhood wounding will ask the pastoral caregiver for prayer. The need may be for a verbal prayer in the moment or for the caregiver to remember the individual in prayer at later times.

With prayer in the moment, the pastoral caregiver has a prime opportunity to communicate in words the understanding of God as loving, empowering, liberating, and redeeming. With personalized prayer encompassing the felt spiritual needs of the parishioner, the caregiver is able to mediate the individual's movement closer to the immanent presence of God.

When a parishioner asks the pastor to pray for her or him at later times, the pastor needs to follow through on the promise to do so. This more private prayer keeps the spiritual needs of the parishioner close to the heart of the pastor and affirms the caregiver's role as a mediator of God's comprehensive love.

The Suffering Servant in the Community

Often, adult survivors of childhood trauma who have come through a lengthy process of healing feel the need to return something to the community, to "give back" some of what they have received. This giving back can complete the circle of redemption, as the parishioner passes on wholeness to others who are wounded, others who receive the opportunity of themselves in turn passing on the healing, and so forth. Pastoral care can encourage the wounded healer impulse as actualizing the image of God.

Usually the careseeker has an idea of how she or he wants to return healing to the community. In these cases, the pastoral caregiver helps the parishioner work through the ideas and supports the parishioner in putting the ideas into action. Redemptive healing can be returned to the community through volunteering, writing, speaking out in the presence of injustice, sharing the story of trauma and recovery with others, becoming involved in church or community groups, and so on.

Deborah remained active in her ALANON group after eight years, even when she didn't necessarily feel the need for the program anymore. She continued out of a conviction that she wanted to be there for others, to give back what was given to her.

Peter wanted to help families who suffered from the "curse" of domestic violence. He donated time in fund-raising and community outreach for a local shelter for abused women and children. He also donated money regularly to a local veterans' group, earmarking the donations for counseling services for vets and their families. In this way he believed he might make a small difference in the lives of families who suffered the way his family had.

Jennifer, at college, became involved in a political group of women fighting sexual violence. She participated in a seminar that trained her to be part of a speakers' team that went to local schools and organizations with the message that sexual violence against women and girls must be obliterated.

Jean, remembering the Christmastimes when the only gifts for the family came from the Salvation Army, established a tradition of buying a bicycle every Christmas for a Salvation Army child.

David, who had felt isolated and powerless during his mother's prolonged bouts with depression, decided to make a career move into social work. He hoped to work with adolescents, consolidating healing of his own inner child in the process.

Giving back to the community restores the sacred within the adult child in several ways. First, the giving reinforces the spiritual growth by actualizing a religiously grounded hope and making operational a theology of grace and compassion. Second, returning the wholeness to the community restores the sacred within by passing on a legacy of redemption.

CONCLUSION

The work of pastoral care with adult survivors of childhood domestic trauma is a considerable undertaking and entails considerable labor. The pastoral caregiver will experience feeling overwhelmed by the stories of suffering, feeling helpless in the face of the injustices done to children, feeling concerned as the individual confronts and exorcises internal demons, feeling challenged in her or his own practical theology as the parishioner struggles to wrest sacred meaning from the pain, and feeling humbled by the power of the holy in restoring lives.

Pastoral care with survivors of domestic trauma is a labor of consuming intensity. Yet it is also an undertaking of tremendous fulfillment and reward. Although feeling overwhelmed, the caregiver also feels honored to be trusted with the telling of the story. Although feeling helpless, the caregiver also feels an empowering righteous anger in the face of injustice. Although feeling concerned, the caregiver also feels pride in the individual's strength and courage in confronting offenders and exorcising internal demons. Although feeling challenged, the caregiver also feels that she or he has been given a gift in the walk toward sacred meaning making. And although feeling humbled by the power of the holy, the caregiver also feels a powerful confirmation of redeeming faith.

Parishioner and pastoral caregiver together glimpse the new heavens and new earth in stepping off the road of domestic trauma and cutting a new path.

appendix

Sample Guided Meditations

The following guided meditations can be used by the pastoral care provider in several ways. The meditations can be read aloud to guide the careseeker in the office setting; the meditations can be recorded on a cassette tape (by the caregiver or the careseeker) for the individual to listen to at home; or the printed meditations can be given to the person as a guideline for meditation at home.

In leading a guided meditation, the pastoral caregiver needs to speak slowly and gently, communicating a sense of peace and safety through her or his voice. Pauses (marked in the following sample meditations with "[pause]," which should not be read aloud) might be from fifteen to thirty seconds in length. It should be noted that there is no right or wrong, good or bad careseeker response to the guided imagery.

INTRODUCTORY WORDS

Each meditation should begin with words guiding the parishioner into a state of relaxation, as follows:

> Close your eyes and breathe slowly and deeply. Breathe in peace, breathe out tension. Feel warmth and security wash over your body. Head to toes. Breathe in and out, in and out. Breathe in peace, breathe out tension. Like calm waves rolling in and out with each breath, feel peace and warmth wash through your body.
>
> Feel yourself relaxing. Let all of the tension flow from your body. Feel your feet relaxing. And your legs. Your torso. Your arms and

hands. Let the tension flow from your neck, and feel the muscles ease. Feel your head relax. Continue to breathe slowly and deeply. In and out. In and out.

In a moment, you will travel on a guided imagery, leaving behind, for the time being, cares or concerns, leaving behind, for the time being, any pressures or stress. You will travel to a special place of warmth and peace, a place of deepened spirituality.

MEETING THE OFFENDER OF THE PAST: "EXORCISING THE INTERNAL DEMON"

In this guided imagery, the notation "[name]" should be filled in with the name of, or phrase describing, the offender: "your father," "your mother," "your brother," for example. In this sample exercise, the name is given masculine pronouns, which of course need to be changed when the wounder was female.

After the initial words of guided relaxation given earlier, the pastoral caregiver continues as follows:

You are moving on a journey to a place special to you. A place where you feel a sense of calm and peace. You are moving to your "safe place." As you get closer, you begin to smell the air and hear the sounds of your safe place. You feel the anticipation within, body and soul. Pay attention to your inner feelings as you draw nearer to this place of calm. Breathe in peace. Breathe out tension. You are safe here.

You are in your safe place. Look around you and breathe the scents deeply. Feel the air on your cheeks, listen to the sounds around you. Let this place draw you in and surround you with its protection and peace. Nothing can harm you here. You are safe here. [Pause.]

Here you will meet [name] today. He cannot hurt you here. You have the chance to speak your heart to him. He cannot respond until you give him permission to. You are the one in power. You are in control. You are safe.

You see [name] in front of you. Tell him what you need to say. Ask what you need to ask. Let him know how you are feeling. [Pause.] Observe your thoughts now, your emotions now. Observe how your body is feeling.

You are strong. You are safe. You are in control. Breathe in peace. Breathe out tension. [Pause.]

Now give [*name*] permission to respond. He cannot hurt you now. Listen to how he responds. Observe how he looks. Notice the expression on his face. Pay attention to your feelings. [Pause.]

Tell [*name*] how you have changed, how strong you are. Tell him he cannot hurt you anymore. Tell him he has no power over you anymore. [Pause.] Tell [*name*] goodbye. Watch him leave. Notice how you are feeling, emotionally and physically.

You are alone again in your safe place. Breathe in peace. Breathe out tension. You feel safe. You feel strong. In a moment you will leave this place. Take one last look around you, and take in the power of this safe place. You can return anytime you want to. [Pause.]

You begin returning to the here and now. Back into this room. Back into your chair. Breathe slowly and deeply. And when you are ready, you may open your eyes.

RECOVERING THE LOST CHILD: "A LOVING ENCOUNTER WITH THE INNER CHILD"

This guided imagery identifies the inner child as a little girl. The gender may be changed in working with male survivors of childhood wounding. This guided imagery takes the careseeker back to a nonspecific time in early memory. The age can be specified as needed, when the caregiver discerns that a particular childhood age needs revisiting.

The pastoral caregiver begins with the introductory guided meditation for relaxation, then continues as follows:

> You are moving back in time to when you were a little girl. Back and back in time, to when you were just a child. You enter into the world of that little girl, and you see that little girl sitting alone. She does not see you yet. You take a moment to observe her. What does she look like? What is she doing? What does she seem to be feeling? How do you feel toward her? [Pause.]

When you are ready, walk up to the little girl. She is not afraid of you. She trusts you. You are her friend. You sit beside her and take her into your lap, holding her and speaking softly to her. Observe how it feels to hold her. [Pause.]

Talk to this little girl, telling her how special she is, how strong she is, what a good person she is. Tell her what you know she needs to hear from you. [Pause.]

Now the little girl is talking to you. Listen closely to her. What is she saying? What is she asking from you? What is she feeling? And what do you feel as you listen to her? She pours out her heart to you, and you take in the words, with respect and esteem. [Pause.]

Now respond to her. Talk together, heart to heart. Share your feelings with her. And listen for the feelings in her words. [Pause.] You are friends. She is safe with you. [Pause.]

In a moment, you need to leave this place. You hug her and tell her you love her. Let her know that whenever she needs you, she simply needs to ask. She needs only to call out to you. You will hear her. She tells you the same. You say goodbye to each other. [Pause.] Take one last look around you, and take in this special place. You can return whenever you need to.

Now you are coming back in time, back to the present, back to this room, back into your chair. Breathe in peace. Breathe out tension. Breathe slowly and deeply. And when you are ready, you may open your eyes.

REACQUAINTING ONESELF WITH GOD: "THE DOVE: BURDEN AND GIFT"

After the introductory relaxation imagery, the pastor continues as follows:

You find yourself walking along a path toward a special place. Follow the path. The path will take you there. As you get closer, you begin to smell the air and hear the sounds of this safe place. Pay attention to your innermost feelings as you draw nearer to this place of calm.

And now you have arrived. Look about you and breathe the scents deeply. Feel the air on your cheeks, and listen to the silence. This place draws you in and surrounds you with its peace.

It dawns on you that you are not alone. A wise, holy presence is with you. You are able to see this presence, in the form of a dove. The dove is here especially for you. You communicate with the dove, a dialogue back and forth. Ask questions, listen, understand. [Pause.]

Notice your sensations. Your toes and your fingers, your face. Breathe slowly and deeply. See all about you, pick up the scents of the air, listen to the sounds. Notice what you are feeling. [Pause.]

The dove wants to lift a burden from you. The dove asks you to leave the burden at its feet. You feel the weight and the heaviness you have been carrying with you. The dove asks you to let it go and to leave it here. You let down the burden. Feel the release. [Pause.]

Now the dove offers you a gift. What is it the dove gives you? Receive the gift and ponder the gift. What is this gift about? How will you use this gift? Why this gift? Why you? [Pause.]

In a moment you will leave this place. You thank the dove. Tell the dove goodbye. The dove invites you to return whenever you need to. Take one last look around you, and take in this special place. [Pause.]

You begin taking the path back. You begin walking back toward the here and now, back into this room, back into your chair. And as you are ready, you may open your eyes.

Notes

INTRODUCTION: CUTTING A NEW PATH

1. Maya Angelou, *Wouldn't Take Nothing for My Journey Now* (New York: Random House, 1993), 24.

2. See the American Association of Pastoral Counselors, "Petition" (presented to Hillary Rodham Clinton on behalf of health care reform) (Fairfax, Va.: American Association of Pastoral Counselors, 1993), 1.

1. IDENTIFYING VICTIM-SURVIVORS

1. Janet Woititz, *Adult Children of Alcoholics* (Pompano Beach, Fla.: Health Communications, 1983), chap. 2.

2. Melody Beattie, *Codependent No More* (New York: Harper and Row, 1987), 188.

3. American Psychiatric Association, *Diagnostic Criteria from DSM-IV* (Washington, D.C.: American Psychiatric Association, 1994), 209–11.

2. THE CAREGIVER'S ROLE

1. Robert Coles, *The Spiritual Life of Children* (Boston: Houghton Mifflin, 1990), 301.

2. Ibid., 304.

3. Carrie Doehring, *Taking Care: Monitoring Power Dynamics and Relational Boundaries in Pastoral Care and Counseling* (Nashville: Abingdon, 1995).

4. American Association of Pastoral Counselors, *Handbook* (Fairfax, Va.: American Association of Pastoral Counselors, 1994), sec. 3, par. E.

3. PARADOXES OF VALUE

1. Merle Jordan, *Taking on the Gods: The Task of the Pastoral Counselor* (Nashville: Abingdon, 1986), 34–35.

2. Claudia Black, *It Will Never Happen to Me* (Denver: Mac Publishing, 1982).

3. Marie Fortune, *Sexual Violence: The Unmentionable Sin* (New York: Pilgrim, 1983), 211.

4. Wendy Maltz and Beverly Holman, *Incest and Sexuality* (Lexington, Mass.: Lexington Books, 1987), 31.

5. See Ruth Duck, ed., *Flames of the Spirit* (New York: Pilgrim, 1985), 71.

4. MYTHS OF THE VICTIM SURVIVOR

1. Rodney Hunter, ed., *Dictionary of Pastoral Care and Counseling* (Nashville: Abingdon, 1990), 771.

2. Rudolf Bultmann, *Jesus Christ and Mythology* (New York: Scribner's, 1958), 18.

3. Ibid., 84.

5. BREAKING THE SILENCE, TELLING THE STORY

1. Judith Herman, *Trauma and Recovery* (New York: Basic, 1992), 178.

2. Dayl Hufford, "How to Break the Cycle of Child Sexual Abuse: Local Churches Can Take Responsibility," *United Church News*, 15 October 1993, 2.

3. Linda Meyer Williams, "Recall of Childhood Trauma: A Prospective Study of Women's Memories of Child Sexual Abuse," in *Journal of Consulting and Clinical Psychology* 62 (1994): 1167–76.

4. Judith Herman and Emily Schatzow, "Recovery and Verification of Childhood Sexual Trauma" (paper presented at the annual meeting of the American Psychiatric Association, Washington, D.C., May 1986), 21.

5. Annie Dillard, *Pilgrim at Tinker Creek* (New York: Harper and Row, 1974), 3.

6. CONFRONTING WOUNDERS OF THE PAST

1. Michael Kerr, "Family Systems Theory and Therapy," in *Handbook of Family Therapy*, ed. Alan Gurman and David Kniskern (New York: Brunner/Mazel, 1981), 256.

2. Anne Wilson Schaef, *When Society Becomes an Addict* (San Francisco: Harper and Row, 1987), 131.

8. RECOVERING THE LOST CHILD

1. Bernie Siegel, *Peace, Love, and Healing* (New York: Harper and Row, 1989), 186.

2. Alice Miller, *For Your Own Good* (New York: Farrar, Straus, and Giroux, 1983), 279.

3. Dillard, *Pilgrim at Tinker Creek,* 90.

4. Thomas Moore, *Care of the Soul: A Guide for Cultivating Depth and Sacredness in Everyday Life* (New York: HarperCollins, 1992), 135.

5. Coles, *Spiritual Life of Children,* 108.

9. RESTORING THE SACRED

1. Dillard, *Pilgrim at Tinker Creek,* 7.

2. United Methodist Church, *The United Methodist Book of Worship* (Nashville: United Methodist Publishing House, 1992), 613–14.

3. Ibid., 621.

4. Howard Clinebell, *Growing through Grief: Personal Healing* (Nashville: UMCom Productions, 1984), videocassette series.

Selected Bibliography

American Association of Pastoral Counselors. *Handbook.* Fairfax, Va.: American Association of Pastoral Counselors, 1994.

———. "Petition." (Presented to Hillary Clinton on behalf of health care reform.) Fairfax, Va.: American Association of Pastoral Counselors, 1993.

American Psychiatric Association. *Diagnostic Criteria from DMS-IV.* Washington, D.C.: American Psychiatric Association, 1994.

Angelou, Maya. *Wouldn't Take Nothing for My Journey Now.* New York: Random House, 1993.

Beattie, Melody. *Codependent No More.* New York: Harper and Row, 1987.

Black, Claudia. *It Will Never Happen to Me.* Denver: Mac Publishing, 1982.

Bultmann, Rudolf. *Jesus Christ and Mythology.* New York: Scribner's, 1958.

Clinebell, Howard. *Growing through Grief: Personal Healing.* Nashville: UMCom Productions, 1984. Videocassette series.

Coles, Robert. *The Spiritual Life of Children.* Boston: Houghton Mifflin, 1990.

Dillard, Annie. *Pilgrim at Tinker Creek.* New York: Harper and Row, 1974.

Doehring, Carrie. *Taking Care: Monitoring Power Dynamics and Relational Boundaries in Pastoral Care and Counseling.* Nashville: Abingdon, 1995.

Duck, Ruth, ed. *Flames of the Spirit.* New York: Pilgrim , 1985.

Esquivel, Laura. *Like Water for Chocolate.* Translated by C. Christensen and T. Christensen. New York: Doubleday, 1992.

Fortune, Marie. *Sexual Violence: The Unmentionable Sin.* New York: Pilgrim, 1983.

Godwin, Gail. *Father Melancholy's Daughter.* New York: William Morrow and Co., 1991.

Guest, Judith. *Ordinary People.* New York: Viking, 1976.

Herman, Judith. *Trauma and Recovery.* New York: Basic, 1992.

Herman, Judith, and Emily Schatzow. "Recovery and Verification of Childhood Sexual Trauma." Paper presented at the annual meeting of the American Psychiatric Association, Washington, D.C. May 1986.

Hufford, Dayl. "How to Break the Cycle of Child Sexual Abuse: Local Churches Can Take Responsibility." *United Church News,* 15 October 1993.

Hunter, Rodney, ed. *Dictionary of Pastoral Care and Counseling*. Nashville: Abingdon, 1990.
Jordan, Merle. *Taking on the Gods: The Task of the Pastoral Counselor*. Nashville: Abingdon, 1986.
Kerr, Michael. "Family Systems Theory and Therapy." In *Handbook of Family Therapy*, edited by Alan Gurman and David Kniskern, 226–64. New York: Brunner/Mazel, 1981.
Maltz, Wendy, and Beverly Holman. *Incest and Sexuality*. Lexington, Mass.: Lexington Books, 1987.
Miller, Alice. *For Your Own Good*. New York: Farrar, Straus, and Giroux, 1983.
Moore, Thomas. *Care of the Soul: A Guide for Cultivating Depth and Sacredness in Everyday Life*. New York: HarperCollins, 1992.
Schaef, Anne Wilson. *When Society Becomes an Addict*. San Francisco: Harper and Row, 1987.
Siegel, Bernice. *Peace, Love, and Healing*. New York: Harper and Row, 1989.
United Methodist Church. *The United Methodist Book of Worship*. Nashville: United Methodist Publishing House, 1992.
Williams, Linda Meyer. "Recall of Childhood Trauma: A Prospective Study of Women's Memories of Child Sexual Abuse." In *Journal of Consulting and Clinical Psychology* 62 (1994): 1167–76.
Woititz, Janet. *Adult Children of Alcoholics*. Pompano Beach, Fla.: Health Communications, 1983.